"WHEN YE PRAY..."

THE ANATOMY OF PRAYER

BOOK TWO

PRAYERS OF THE OLD TESTAMENT

VOLUME ONE

MICHAEL BOLDEA, JR.

BOLDMAN PUBLISHING
WATERTOWN, WISCONSIN

WATERTOWN, WISCONSIN

Published by
Boldman Publishing
Watertown, Wisconsin

http://www.handofhelp.com

ISBN-13: 978-1519366351

All Scripture taken from the New King James edition.

Cover Photo: Michael Boldea, Jr. A church near the famous cathedral in Alba Iulia, Romania on a winter's evening.

TABLE OF CONTENTS

Romans 15:4, "For whatever things were written before were written for our learning, that we through the patience and comfort of the Scriptures might have hope."

INTRODUCTION

It would be a cumbersome thing to have to reinvent the wheel every morning upon waking. While the wise man builds upon the things built by those who came before him, a foolish man dismisses all that was, thinking himself the pinnacle of what is, and making no progress in what is to be. The Word of God was given to us that we might learn from the lessons left by those who came before us. Among the many lessons the men and women of God left for us, we discover the lessons derived from their prayer lives and even the very prayers they prayed to be plentiful, challenging, enlightening and educational.

Since all true men and women of God are individuals for whom prayer is a vital need, and the Bible is rife with men and women of God, it is no surprise that we find a multitude of prayers within the pages of Scripture. Whether short prayers or long, whether for strength, protection, wisdom, boldness, victory, guidance, and a myriad of other things, the prayers those of the Old Testament prayed – prayers subsequently answered of God in amazing ways – are ours to peruse and study and learn from.

We are a blessed generation not because we are more technologically advanced than our predecessors, but because these technological advancements give us greater access to the Word of God, and greater insights regarding every conceivable facet of the Scriptures.

Have you ever wondered why some prayers were included within the pages of Scripture while others are forever forgotten by all but God? Have you ever wondered why less prominent individuals' prayers are recounted in the Bible word for word, while men of great import and their pleas toward God are nowhere to be found?

If we believe God to be sovereign–and we do because His Word tell us that He is–then we know that neither what was included or omitted from the pages of Scripture was in any way accidental, but rather everything that's in the Word is there for a purpose…the purpose being our understanding.

We learn by reading the Word of God, and God included everything He wanted us to know in His word because of this. So if the prayers of Abraham, Jacob, Moses, Joshua, Jabez, Hannah, Samuel, David, Solomon, Elijah, Ezra, or Nehemiah are included in the Bible, our duty is to discover why, and what it is we can learn from their prayers.

Why did these men and women of God pray? When did these men and women of God pray? How did these men and women of God pray? Where did these men and women of God pray? All these questions are relevant and important because they set a precedent, and we know that the God who changes not can move on our behalf just as He moved on their behalf.

What stirred the heart of God in these individuals' prayers? What caused God to heed the cries and petitions of these individuals? Was it the words themselves, or was it something more? Was it just the attitude of the heart, the faith they possessed, or some as yet unquantifiable virtue that caused the sea to part, the sun to stand still, or fire to come down from heaven and consume an altar and the sacrifice upon it?

There is much ground to cover, many prayers to meditate upon and search out, because although I will include his prayer in this book series, there is more to prayer than the prayer of Jabez, and prayer itself is a more complex issue than the handful of words Jabez uttered.

We are taught to pray by four distinct means. First, the Holy Spirit teaches us to pray, stirring in us the words we must speak, and giving us the unction to do so. Second, Christ Himself teaches us to pray, as He taught His disciples to pray, giving us an outline of the type of prayer received and accepted of God. Third, the Bible teaches us how to pray, giving us various examples. And fourth, the lives of those who came before us, and their petitions and supplications before God teach us how to pray, and this is why it is a worthwhile and profitable endeavor to acquaint ourselves with the prayers of the forefathers of the faith, those toward whom we look and behold as giants, even though they were average, ordinary human beings.

We model our prayer lives, learn what we ought to pray for, and how we ought to pray by looking to those who came before us as examples, and role models. We also learn how not to pray, and what not to pray for in certain cases, and because balance is a core principal of any endeavor, we will discuss this aspect of prayer and the afferent examples as well.

The beauty of God's Word is that within its pages we discover all we need in order to have a fruitful, vibrant, animated, and fulfilling spiritual life. God leaves nothing to chance, nor does He veil anything that ought to be revealed. Given enough time, patience, prayer, and dedication you will discover the answer to every important question within the Bible.

'Whatever things were written before were written for our learning,' so if we fail to learn, it is not God's fault but our own for not having diligently sought out the Scriptures.

Since learning is a process and not something that can take place instantaneously, our journey into the land of prayer, and all that it entails, continues with the second part of what I hope will be a five part treatise on prayer.

In part one, we discovered what prayer was, and came to understand it. What follows, is an in-depth look at the prayers prayed throughout the Old Testament which will be broken up into two volumes followed by two more volumes of a diligent study of the prayers prayed throughout the New Testament.

Although it is a grace not to have to reinvent the wheel, it is still necessary to know what a wheel is, what it does, how it works, and why it works so well.

Genesis 18:23, "And Abraham came near and said, 'Would you also destroy the righteous with the wicked?'"

CHAPTER ONE
THE PRAYER OF ABRAHAM

E ver since I could remember, I've always thought of Abraham as the first intercessor. If we study the Word of God with diligence, we realize Abraham was the first man to stand in the gap for a people, the first to intercede on behalf of not one but two cities which had forsaken all that was moral and decent, and who had given themselves over to the lusts of their flesh. It was not for the sake of the reprobate and those who practiced their grievous sin unhindered that Abraham interceded; it was for the righteous within the city that he pleaded time and again.

God informed Abraham as to what was about to happen to the cities of Sodom and Gomorrah. As God often does, He forewarns and foreshadows that which He is soon to do, informing His beloved well ahead of time concerning what is to come. As we will soon see, the notion of God revealing future events is not something new, but has been around since the beginning of recorded history, when He revealed to Noah that He would punish the world and the sin therein by flood.

God does not hide what He is doing from His children. The only ones who ought to be ignorant of God's plans are those who do not know God, and have no relationship with Him. Tragically however, more and more believers today are ignorant of what God has planned, because their rational mind refuses to believe that God still communicates with His children on such an intimate level.

The angels of the Lord had appeared to Abraham by the terebinth trees of Mamre, and they were three in number. Abraham treated them kindly, taking butter and milk and a calf which he prepared, and setting it before them, and they ate.

After telling Sarah she would have a child even though she had passed the age of child bearing, the men rose from there, looked toward Sodom, and Abraham went with them to send them on their way.

Genesis 18:17-19, "And the Lord said, 'shall I hide from Abraham what I am doing, since Abraham shall surely become a great and mighty nation, and all the nations of the earth shall be blessed in him? For I have known him, in order that he may command his children and his household after him, that they keep the way of the Lord, to do righteousness and justice, that the Lord may bring to Abraham what He has spoken to him."

What an honor it is for God to say, 'I have known him' of a man. God didn't pick Abraham randomly; He didn't just close his eyes and point to someone roaming about the earth. He knew Abraham, knew that he kept the way of the Lord, and that he did righteousness and justice. God knew the character of Abraham, long before He communed with him, and sent His messengers to him.

Because God knew Abraham, He knew he could not keep His plans from him.

Genesis 18:20-21, "And the Lord said, 'because the outcry against Sodom and Gomorrah is great, and because their sin is very grievous, I will go down now and see whether they have done altogether according to the outcry against it that has come to Me; and if not, I will know."

It's almost as though God couldn't quite believe what He was hearing concerning Sodom and Gomorrah. Although the outcry against Sodom and Gomorrah was great, the Lord had decided to go down and see whether or not the citizenry of these two cities had done altogether according to the outcry against them, or if there had been some exaggeration along the way.

God classified the outcry against Sodom and Gomorrah and the sin they were accused of committing, as very grievous. Since the word grievous means serious, dire, heinous or severe, we understand that these were no run-of-the-mill, ordinary, every-day shortcomings, but something horrid enough wherein it warranted the Lord's personal investigation.

What many choose to gloss over is that there was indeed an outcry against Sodom and Gomorrah, so there were still those who saw their sin for what it was and cried out to God.

We are living times very similar to those of Abraham and Lot. Sin has once more peaked, and since God has not changed, without true repentance there is no other conclusion, there is no other possible outcome, than the fate visited upon Sodom and Gomorrah.

If God, however, is yet allowing for a time of grace, if He is still allowing for a season wherein men can still repent, our duty is still to pray that the hearts of the lost might be reached, the righteous might be protected, and the glory of God be made manifest even in His judgment. When it comes to interceding on behalf of others, and praying for others, Abraham's example is a shining one, not only due to the love he showed toward the righteous, but also due to his persistence, his repeated petitions, and his continued leadings even at the risk of wearying God.

The first obvious lesson we can glean from this exchange between the Lord and Abraham, is the implied relationship and intimacy. In order for God to hear our prayers and answer them, there must be a relationship and a fellowship with Him. Abraham was God's friend, and God could not keep hidden what He was about to do because of this.

Before Abraham came before the Lord to plead for the lives of those in Sodom, he was an obedient servant of God who kept the way of the Lord, and did righteousness and justice. Try as one might to say that righteousness and keeping the way of the Lord have no bearing on whether or not He answers our prayers, the Word of God says otherwise. Any relationship, including our relationship with God, must be of a reciprocal nature. If every morning upon waking and every evening upon going to sleep, my wife would greet me with an 'I love you,' and all I'd do is shrug my shoulders and roll my eyes, it would likely have been a short marriage indeed. Reciprocity is key in any relationship, wherein you return the love and affection you are shown in kind.

Abraham had a relationship with God. If we study the prayer of Abraham on behalf of the citizenry of Sodom and Gomorrah, we recognize it was more of a dialogue than anything else. It was a conversation between Abraham and the God of the universe–God who spoke all things into being, and breathed life into the first man.

The very notion that we can stand before this great and mighty God, and speak to Him, have a relationship with Him, fellowship with Him, and commune with Him, is almost too much to wrap our heads around. And yet, God's desire is to have a relationship with His creation, and whenever He finds those with open hearts and humble spirits, He is ever willing to speak to them as a father would to His own child.

Abraham was not reticent in approaching God. He was not fearful, he was not apprehensive, because he knew his God intimately. Abraham knew God personally, and the foundation of fellowship which had been cemented over the years was now stronger than ever. As any relationship or bond forms, Abraham's relationship with God formed over time as Abraham proved his faithfulness and obedience towards God.

Because he was such a looming figure, including being one of the patriarchs, we tend to gloss over Abraham's obedience toward God, which he demonstrated dutifully whenever he was called upon to do so.

Genesis 12:1, "Now the Lord had said to Abram: Get out of your country, from your kindred and from your father's house, to a land that I will show you."

Genesis 12:4, "So Abram departed as the Lord had spoken to him, and Lot went with him. And Abram was seventy-five years old when he departed from Haran."

There are a handful of instances in the Bible wherein the obedience of certain servants is highlighted as a testament to us all…this is one of those instances.

Abraham was seventy-five years old when God spoke to him and commanded him to leave his country, everything he'd known, everything he was used to, and go to a land that God would subsequently show him at a later date. No matter how much one might comb through the Bible to find Abraham complaining or asking more questions concerning this command, they won't find it because it isn't there.

God did not reveal His entire plan to Abraham. He simply told him to get out of his country and go, and He would show him the place where he ought to settle in at a later date. Abraham didn't have the entire plan, he didn't see the entire picture, but he trusted God enough to know that He wouldn't fail him, or abandon him halfway through his journey. When we have formed a relationship with someone, we learn to trust them implicitly. We don't ask questions, we just do as they ask knowing that if they're asking a certain thing of us there must be a good reason.

If the foundation of a solid relationship did not exist between Abraham and God, do you really think he would have picked up and left the only land he'd ever known at the age of seventy-five without asking any questions whatsoever? Abraham knew God would not lead him astray. Abraham knew God had a plan and a purpose, and that only by obeying the voice of God would he see the plan and purpose of God unfolding before his very eyes.

Most of us like to know where we're going before we start any sort of journey. Even before we pack our bags, even before we make plans for the pets, even before we ask someone to water our plants or check in on the house, we have a destination in mind. Whether it's a week long getaway or a weekend trip into the mountains, we want to know where we're going, where we're going to be staying once we get there, and even what route we're going to be taking to our destination.

Imagine how difficult it must have been for Abraham to start a journey having no clue of his final destination, knowing he would not be returning to his homeland ever again. God didn't send Abraham on vacation. He didn't say 'go, hang out for a couple weeks, see if you like it, and if the weather meets with your approval then we'll talk.'

God told Abraham to get out of his country, away from his kindred, and out of his father's house, and He would tell him his destination at a later date. What Abraham did took trust and faith, two essential ingredients for a true and lasting relationship with God.

When we trust God, and have faith that He will lead us to green pastures, He will often require us to get out of our comfort zones. Many a time we do not see the fulfillment of God's plan in our lives, because we did not obey a certain command along the way, or we dragged our feet awaiting further explanation, or firmer details. If God says 'go,' then go...you will eventually receive further instructions when the time comes, but first you must carry out the initial order of actually going.

If we do not truly know God, we will never obey such life altering commands as leaving behind everything we've ever known and heading off to a strange land. This is why building and nurturing a relationship with Him is so vital and paramount. Do we do as God commands? Do we obey the voice of the Lord? The key to Abraham's effectiveness in prayer, as well as the level of intimacy he shared with God, is applied obedience. There is a difference between the theory of obedience, and the practice of obedience. Applied obedience is the theory turned to practice, and it is something we as believers must endeavor to remain in, into perpetuity.

We cannot be selective when it comes to obeying God. We cannot obey simply what we deem beneficial or profitable, or those things with a low level of difficulty. Obedience is a must even in difficult circumstances; it is a must even when God asks the difficult things of us, because we know the end result is for our good, our growth, and our maturing.

We have close to one hundred children in our orphanage, so I could only imagine how maddening it would be for the staff if the children only obeyed them fifty percent of the time. If you have children, perhaps you can relate and understand how God feels when we selectively obey Him, choosing to ignore Him in certain areas, or when it comes to doing certain things.

Nowadays everyone wants God to hear and answer their prayers, while simultaneously desiring to be able to ignore certain times when God is speaking to them. Such a mindset does not a relationship make, and if there is no relationship between us and God, then we cannot hope to dialogue or fellowship with Him as we would desire.

Proverbs 1:24-25, "Because I have called and you refused, I have stretched out my hand and no one regarded, because you disdain all my counsel, and would have none of my reproof, I also will laugh at your calamity; I will mock when your terror comes, when your terror comes like a storm, and your destruction comes like a whirlwind, when distress and anguish come upon you."

Disobedience is not inconsequential! Throughout the Word of God we see the consequences of disobedience, and they are, without fail, always dire. We cannot refuse the call of God, disdain His counsel, reject His reproof, disregard His stretched out hand, and still expect Him to save us from calamity, and shield us from the terror when it comes like a storm.

There are countless souls walking about today thinking themselves sons and daughters of God, whom God has never known. Men and women, who at best are illegitimate children, and who at worst are self-deceived individuals who expect God to bend to their will and not the other way around. Such individuals never bothered to be still and hear the voice of the Lord, they never bothered to receive His correction and walk the paths of righteousness, yet they expect and feel entitled to God's protection and sanctuary whenever distress and anguish come upon the world.

We cannot love what God abhors, receive what God rejects, embrace what God spews out, then still live with the expectation that when the time comes He will save us from the midst of destruction. If we are of God, then we love what He loves, hate what He hates, embrace what He embraces, and obey what He commands. It's that simple! It's not complicated! Men, however, attempt to complicate the truth, and in the process water it down for fear that those who would receive the undiluted, unadulterated truth are too few to support their lavish lifestyles and propensity for the finer things in life.

Because they place their own wants, lusts, and comfort above the saving of men's souls, they wholly disregard the words of Jesus, who spoke of the narrow path and the few who find it, and who spoke of the many called and the few who were chosen.

Proverbs 1:28-31, "Then they will call on me, but I will not answer; they will seek me diligently, but they will not find me. Because they hated knowledge and did not choose the fear of the Lord, they would have none of my counsel and despised all my reproof, therefore they shall eat the fruit of their own way, and be filled to the full with their own fancies."

Obedience is a choice, as is the fear of the Lord. Depending on what we choose, we will either walk in the protection of almighty God, or eat the fruit of our own way. It is and always has been an either/or proposition, and the Word of God is clear on this matter, as it is clear on so many matters which seem to be an issue with some believers. Yes, the day will come when men will call on God, and He will not answer, when they will seek Him diligently but not find Him. That day is fast approaching, and no man can stop it.

Love knowledge, receive the counsel of the Lord, esteem the reproof of God, and choose the fear of the Lord, that He may know you as His own, and keep you in the days of darkness. We've been preaching butterflies and lollipops for so long, that when the Lord does reprove us, we bristle and conclude it couldn't possibly be Him, because we were never told that God chastens His children.

Although man continues to try and redefine God, making Him in their image with each subsequent try, God remains the great I Am, and no amount of philosophical red herrings and no amount of feelings, will change who God is. As individuals we choose obedience, we choose the fear of the Lord, we choose to receive the counsel of God, and for these things we will receive our just reward when that Day of Days is upon us. Just remember, all those lovely people with the bright smile and the private jets that insistently tell you God has changed, will neither be able to, nor have any inclination toward lifting a finger in helping you when the day of terror comes like a storm.

We are wrought with indecision because although the Word of God, our conscience, and our instincts tell us one thing, men who've been attending seminaries for decades, have degrees in Hebrew and Greek, and shepherd congregations of thousands tells us otherwise. The inner conflict arises when we give heed to anyone other than Christ, and the Word of God, allowing contradictory viewpoints into our heart because we've been conditioned to hear all sides of the story before we make a decision.

The devil is a liar...that's all the story I need to know. Knowing that our enemy is the great deceiver, and he's been at this for millennia, it is logical to conclude that if you hear him out, if you give him the time, he will do his utmost to cause you to stray from truth. Sadly, in many cases he even succeeds in drawing individuals away from the love and grace of Christ, and this is evident in all the aberrant pseudo-Christian denominations still sprouting up like fungi after a summer rain.

In a hundred yard journey, being off by one degree doesn't really make much of a difference. In a ten thousand mile journey, however, being off course by one degree can very well put you in another country, if not on another continent. The point is that this journey we are on is not for a day or a week...it is a lifelong journey and any deviation from the path, even one as small as one degree can have dire consequences at the end of it. The enemy isn't trying to get believers to become atheists, he's just trying to get them to believe Jesus can do, or does, less than He promises, thereby doubting the Christ Himself, and allowing uncertainty and unbelief to take root in the heart.

The enemy we face is by no means new at this, and he has made an art form of subtleness and finesse. 'Hey, come on now, do you really believe Jesus turned water into wine, or walked on water? Don't you think it made more sense if these things were symbolic representations of lessons He was attempting to teach?'

'Hey, come on now, do you really think the Holy Spirit descended on the day of Pentecost and filled one hundred and twenty people with some sort of power? Don't you think it made more sense if by the Holy Spirit Jesus really meant our conscience?'

And so, one thing leads to another, baby step follows baby step until we find ourselves in the wilderness, surrounded by wolves, having only an NIV Bible and a pack of Twizzlers for defense. One of the worst things to happen to the household of faith within the last hundred years is that we came to believe we could let others fight our battles for us. 'Why tire yourself out? Why spend count-less nights in prayer, reading the Word, praying for power, when for a small fee we will do the fighting for you?' It seemed like such a great deal until those we hired to fight our battles took our money and ran, and since we'd gotten so comfortable just being static, and altogether rusty from not raising a sword in years, we decided it was more profitable to wave the white flag of surrender.

Since the beginning of time men of God understood, and inherently so, that no one can fight your battles for you, and if you are called to stand on the front lines, sending a surrogate just won't cut it.

Another aspect of their relationship with God, something all true servants understood and understand to this day, is the need for obedience, whether the task set before us is great or small. God does not look at the size of the task He assigns us; His only concern is if it was carried out or not. Some today, look upon their assigned tasks and refuse to do them because they deem them beneath their level of wisdom, understanding or notoriety. They refuse obedience be-cause they feel as though God should have called them to something greater, not realizing that whatever God has called you to, wherever He has called you to, is where He needs you at that particular mo-ment.

There are others still, who attempt general obedience when-ever God tells them to do a certain, specific thing. They take it upon themselves to improve upon what God has commanded, as though He needed help, or they knew better than He. Although a gilded chariot is more bombastic than a glass of water, to a man dying of thirst in the desert, it is the glass of water that he would prize above ten gilded chariots.

Do what God tells you to do, be aware of the details, and fol-low His instructions to the letter. He knows best…He always has, and He always will.

Not only did Abraham obey God, he also believed God. Doubt, in its many forms, is the bane of the Christian experience. We start to stand on faith, only to allow the enemy to sow seeds of doubt in our hearts, and if they are not quickly and permanently exterminated, they grow, and bloom, and choke off the faith we once had altogether. Before you can bend the knee and petition God for anything, you must first determine whether or not you possess faith that your prayer will be answered. Prayer is an act of faith. Absent faith, prayer is just you and I talking to the ceiling. If you lack faith, then first and foremost pray for faith, then once you know you have come into possession of it, petition God for other things. Faith is a crucial element of prayer, one that Abraham not only possessed, but demonstrated frequently.

As Abraham was growing advanced in his age, and he saw the possibility of having children dwindling with every breath he drew, he came before the Lord pouring out his heart, reminding Him that though God had blessed him, all he possessed would be left to Eliezer of Damascus, a man born in his house, but not of his blood.

Genesis 15:4-6, "And behold the word of the Lord came to him, saying, 'This one shall not be your heir, but one who will come from your own body shall be your heir. Then He brought him outside and said, 'Look now toward heaven, and count the stars if you are able to number them.' And He said to him, 'So shall your descendants be.' And he believed in the Lord and He accounted it to him for righteousness."

God speaks to Abraham, and tells him that his descendants will be as numerous as the stars in the heavens. Seeing as Abraham had no children at this moment in time, it might have seemed improbable, if not outright impossible for this to come to pass, yet Abraham believed in the Lord. If God promises something, even if to human reason it might seem impossible, it will come to pass because God promised it. Abraham believed! He didn't ask how, when, or if God was certain of this lofty promise...he just believed.

Far too often, when God promises us something, it seems we require further explanation. We want God to confirm His promise, thrice if possible, then go about telling us the steps by which He will fulfill said promise in our lives. We obsess over the details so much, we see the impossibility of it by filtering it through human reason, that at some point along the way we begin to doubt, and because we doubt it, the promise does not come to pass. When the promise of God doesn't come to pass because we doubted, we shrug our shoulders and in the back of our minds think to ourselves, 'I knew it couldn't happen; I knew it was too much even for God to do.'

I work in a ministry toward which God made some truly wondrous promises. I was there when these promises were spoken through vessels with the gift of prophecy, and even in our darkest hour, when things seemed bleakest, I did not for one second doubt the veracity of the words our ministry had received. Yes, in the natural these words seemed improbable, even impossible, but our God is not constrained by the natural. He is a supernatural God, and performs supernatural works, and so we cannot limit Him by attempting to put Him in a box of our own making.

Some of those promises have indeed come to pass, others we are still waiting on, but we never ceased to believe the Lord, because the Word of the Lord is true, and He is able to do all things beyond what the human mind can imagine or conceive.

'Abraham, count the stars.'

'They are too many to count Lord.'

'So shall your descendants be.'

And that was the end of the dialogue. Abraham believed, and God kept His promise. Why make things complicated when simple is so much simpler? Just believe God at His Word. Don't try to reason it out, don't try to see the how of it in the physical…just believe.

Because Abraham believed, not only did God keep His promise toward him, the fact that he believed was also accounted to him for righteousness. Abraham's faith was such an inspiring thing, that Paul the Apostle of Christ reminds us of it in his epistle to the Romans as well.

Romans 4:20-21, "He did not waver at the promise of God through unbelief, but was strengthened in faith, giving glory to God, and being fully convinced that what He had promised He was also able to perform."

In two short verses Paul explains what it is to have faith, and uses Abraham as the example we must aspire toward. Having faith is being fully convinced that what God promised, He is able to perform. Are you fully convinced that what God promised you He is able to perform? If the answer is yes, then give glory to God, and thank Him for His faithfulness and goodness.

Men of faith take God at His Word. He promises, and they are fully convinced that He will keep His promise. No matter the circumstances, no matter the odds, no matter the impossibility of the situation, if God promised it, and you are a person of faith, you are convinced that He will carry out His promise. If you are lacking in it, pray for an increase of faith, that you will do as Abraham did and be fully convinced of God's ability to carry out His promise. He is faithful to give us faith when we ask it, for His desire is to see His beloved walk by faith and not by sight.

Abraham was in covenant with God, and God was in covenant with Abraham. A covenant is a clause in a contract that requires one party to do, or refrain from doing certain things. A covenant, as is the case with any contract, requires two parties, and both parties must adhere to the agreed upon terms. As long as Abraham upheld his side of the covenant, God upheld His side of the covenant as well.

Genesis 15:18, "On that same day the Lord made a covenant with Abram, saying."

We are, as Abraham was in covenant with God as well. The covenant we are in was signed and sealed by the blood of the Lamb of God, the Christ, the only begotten. It is a great and wondrous covenant indeed, and if we hope to have our prayers answered, we must uphold and adhere to our part of the covenant, not trampling underfoot the blood of Jesus. The relationship between Abraham and God was also well defined. Abraham knew he was God's servant, God knew He was Abraham's master, and their relationship highlighted this truth.

Yes, nowadays the notion of being a servant, even a servant of God, is unpopular, because it's far more appealing being a master of one's own destiny than a servant beholden to a master...even if that master happens to be God, the creator of all that is. Servitude has become anathema even within the confines of the household of faith, and whenever the subject of servitude is broached, even if it is from a wholly biblical perspective, you can see individuals bristle at the thought, and reject the very notion of it.

Genesis 25:24, "And the Lord appeared to him the same night and said, 'I am the God of your father Abraham; do not fear, for I am with you. I will bless you and multiply your descendants for My servant Abraham's sake."

The Lord appeared to Isaac, Abraham's son, and informed him that for His servant Abraham's sake, God would bless him and multiply his descendants. Although God loves us, and sent Jesus to die on a cross that we might be reconciled unto Him, we must never forget our place, and our duty before an omnipotent God. If God saw Abraham, whom He considered his friend as a servant, are we any closer to Him, or have we built a more profound relationship than Abraham, to see ourselves as anything more?

Whether we want to admit it or not, or acknowledge the veracity of the following statement, every man is a servant of something, and beholden to someone else. We are either servants of light, or servants of darkness...servants of sin or servants of God. We are either beholden to the ruler of this present age, or to God the Father through Christ Jesus His Son. No man is master of his destiny, but every man chooses the master he serves. No man can serve two masters, but neither can a man serve no master at all.

Romans 6:22, "But now having been set free from sin, and having become slaves of God, you have your fruit to holiness, and the end, everlasting life."

We have been set free from sin, to which we were slaves, but once we have been set free from sin, we become slaves of God. I submit to you, God is a far better master than sin will ever be, and this is evidenced by the gift He gives to all His servants, the gift of everlasting life. It was God's servant Abraham who stood in the gap and interceded for Sodom. It was God's servant Abraham who had

His ear to such an extent that he approached God, time and again, beseeching Him to spare the righteous even if they turned out to be no more than a handful.

One of the most important lessons we can learn about servanthood is that a servant serves unconditionally.

A servant submits to the will of his master, without complaint or pretense. A servant does not question nor does a servant do something he was commanded differently than how his master told him to do it. As we have done with so many words in our day and age, we have redefined the word servant, and given it a negative connotation. What so many fail to realize when discussing servanthood and being a servant of God, is that every true man of God was foremost a servant of God, and yes, even a slave of God, who surrendered their will, aspirations, dreams and desires so the will of God might be made manifest through them. Because Abraham was a good and noble servant, he became something more, and achieved a status few in the history of mankind have achieved…that of friend of God.

It takes true, protracted, and consistent intimacy to be called a friend of God, and we begin to understand the relationship between Abraham and God due to the patience and indulgence God showed toward him, as Abraham came before Him repeatedly pleading for Sodom.

Isaiah 41:8, "But you, Israel, are My servant, Jacob, whom I have chosen, the descendants of Abraham My friend."

God is many things, but fickle and forgetful are not among them. Hundreds of years had passed since Abraham had gone back to the earth, yet God remembered His friend, God remembered the bond He had with Abraham, even after all this time. When God forms a bond, it is lasting. When He calls someone His friend, rare as it might be, He really means it, and it is not something that diminishes with time, or is nullified by circumstance.

Think back to how many friends you had growing up, throughout your adolescence, into your teens, and into adulthood. Now see how many of those individuals you still consider friends today. I know there are countless individuals I thought I'd never grow apart from, to whom I haven't talked in at least a decade. Such is the life of man. We grow forgetful, neglectful, we move, we marry, we have children, and things such as friendships, especially those formed in our youth tend to fade. Not so with God. God remembers His friends even after centuries have gone by, because God is neither forgetful, nor reticent in identifying those who were His friends, and continuing to refer to them as such long after they have gone from this earth.

The first, and perhaps most important lesson Abraham teaches us in regards to prayer, is that the individual who prays must first have a relationship with God if they hope to receive an answer to their prayers. There are many benefits to being a servant of God, as well as a friend of God, and having one's prayers answered, is just the tip of a much larger iceberg. May we endeavor to be good and faithful servants, for only through servanthood can one achieve the status of friend of God.

Abraham loved God. This is obvious in his actions and conduct. Abraham loved God not for what God had given him nor for what God had promised to give him, but for who God was. Because Abraham loved God for who He was, and not for what God could do for Him, God counted Abraham as His friend.

Too often men attempt to build a relationship with God having a certain vested interest as the motivator or the driving force behind the desire for intimacy. Since God knows all things, including the intent of the heart and why men do what they do, often times He rejects men's friend requests because their true desire was not friendship with Him, but leveraging the friendship for something else entirely. How would you feel if someone attempted to befriend you only to get something from you? Well, that's the same way God feels when we attempt to cozy up to Him, just to ask for something we might want a little further down the road.

The heart is a duplicitous thing, and all those Scriptures concerning the heart being exceedingly wicked are not exaggerations. God knows the hearts of men better than men know their own hearts, and as He searches the heart, and pierces the heart, weighs the heart, and purifies the heart, He knows exactly what's in it.

Because Abraham's heart was pure before God, because Abraham loved God for whom He was, God counted him as His friend forever.

2 Chronicles 20:7, 'Are You not our God, who drove out the inhabitants of this land before Your people Israel, and gave it to the descendants of Abraham Your friend forever?"

As His friend, God knew He could not keep from Abraham that which He was about to do with Sodom and Gomorrah. As He knows the true meaning of every word, God also knows the true meaning of friend. This was not a one way relationship. It was reciprocal, and as such God shared His plans with Abraham, and Abraham shared his heart with God. Although Abraham is widely considered to be the first intercessor in the Word of God, he is not the first man to be made privy to the plans of God.

We serve a faithful God, who has no desire to leave His children in the dark, or keep them in ignorance. God shares His plans, and foretells us what is to be that we might prepare spiritually, and know He is God, omniscient, over past, present and future when we see what He foretold come to pass.

Genesis 6:13, "And God said to Noah, 'the end of all flesh has come before Me, for the earth is filled with violence through them; and behold, I will destroy them with the earth."

Of those who walked the earth in his day, Noah found grace in the eyes of the Lord, and the Lord told him what He was about to do. Not only did God tell Noah His plan, He also gave him specific instructions concerning the building of an ark, which would be a place of safety for him and his family. Noah could have chosen not to heed the voice of God. He could have pretended not to hear God's instructions, seeing as what God was asking of him was time consuming, labor intensive, and would likely be derided by his contemporaries. Because Noah was a good servant, however, he obeyed the voice of the Lord, and in his obedience he found a place of refuge not only for himself, but also for his family.

Be a friend of God, and you will know what the future holds. Be a friend of God, and He will commune with you and fellowship with you, and speak to you that you might understand His will for your life, and walk in His commandments.

John 15:14-15, "You are my friends if you do whatever I command you. No longer do I call you servants, for a servant does not know what his master is doing; but I have called you friends, for all things that I heard from My Father I have made known to you."

A servant does not know what his master is doing...a friend does. Jesus called His disciples friends, and because they were His friends, He told them all things that He had heard from the Father, and as such they knew what God was doing.

In order to know the plan of God, you must first know God Himself. There are many people today who want to know the plan of God, but have no desire to know Him. They want to know what God is saying, they want to know about prophecy, and dreams, and visions, but when you tell them that the knowledge of things to come, absent a true and vibrant relationship with God, is worthless, they bristle and begin to accuse you of judging them. Abraham knew God, and because he knew God, he was also able to know the plan of God. Because he obeyed God, God considered Abraham His friend, and as such shared His plan with Abraham before carrying it out.

We begin to understand just how intimate Abraham's knowledge of God was, by what He said to God upon being informed that Sodom was about to be destroyed.

Genesis 18:23-25, "And Abraham came near and said, 'would You also destroy the righteous with the wicked? Suppose there were fifty righteous within the city; would You also destroy the place and not spare it for the fifty righteous that were in it? Far be it from you to do such a thing as this, to slay the righteous with the wicked so that the righteous should be as the wicked; far be it from You! Shall not the judge of all the earth do right?'"

'Shall not the judge of all the earth do right?'

Within this handful of words, we see just how well Abraham knew God. Abraham knew God was just, Abraham knew God was righteous, and Abraham knew God was merciful. Abraham understood the nature of God, and within this question we see this truth highlighted. It is a grace and a blessing to understand and know the multidimensionality of God. Often times we get into trouble because we begin to perceive God as one dimensional. Whether all love, all justice, all mercy, all righteousness, whenever we isolate one of God's many attributes and disregard all the rest, we are in essence, fashioning our own god.

Yes, God is love, but He is also righteous. Yes God is just, but He is also merciful. When He chooses to show more mercy than judgment, it is entirely up to Him.

Jonah 3:10, "Then God saw their works, that they turned from their evil way, and God relented from the disaster that He had said He would bring upon them, and He did not do it."

God had thoroughly made up His mind in regards to Nineveh. He had spoken, and had said He would bring a disaster upon the city, but the citizenry of Nineveh did something that stirred the heart of God and stilled His hand of judgment…they repented. The citizenry of Nineveh, from the king on down, turned from their evil way, and God relented from the disaster that He said He would bring upon them. It is because of the repentance that God chose to withhold judgment; it was not because God decided to give Nineveh a pass. This is something we must understand clearly, because many today still live under the misconception that God will withhold judgment simply because we tell Him to.

When God sees repentance, His heart is stirred, and He is quick to forgive, and relent. Notice, the people of Nineveh didn't just say they were sorry, they didn't just admit to wrongdoing, they turned from their evil way. This is true repentance…turning from one's evil way and walking the path of righteousness.

Romans 2:4, "Or do you despise the riches of His goodness, forbearance, and longsuffering, not knowing that the goodness of God leads you to repentance?"

Man either despises the riches of God's goodness, forbearance, and longsuffering, or He sees them as the tools by which God draws and leads him to repentance. If we see them as the goodness of God that leads us to repentance, then action is required on our part, namely the act of carrying out the repentance to which we were led.

If we read this passage carefully, we see that the goodness of God leads us to repentance, but it cannot impose or force repentance upon us. Repentance is something we as individuals must practice. It is something we as individuals initiate and it is something God honors whenever we do it. Not only do we see the friendship and close bond Abraham had with God, not only do we see how intimately Abraham knew God, we also come to understand Abraham's heart from the prayer he prayed.

You can tell a lot about a man by how he prays for others, and how he intercedes on behalf of others. Abraham was a man whose heart beat for the lost. Though he did not know them personally, though he disliked Sodom enough to live far from it, Abraham still came before God and prayed on their behalf, asking the Lord to spare the righteous of the city. Abraham was safe. He was far from Sodom, in his own tents, being tended to by his servants, and living his life. Abraham had no vested interest. He had not invested in Sodom's real estate, he hadn't put up apartment buildings he was hoping to sell, there was no hidden agenda, or external motivation for Abraham to intercede on behalf of Sodom, than his righteous, loving heart.

Upon hearing the news that Sodom would be judged, Abraham could have reacted very differently than how he did react. He could have shrugged his shoulders and asked, 'what is it to me?' He could have nodded his head in approval and said, 'good, that's what they deserve!', but instead, Abraham came before the Lord asking Him to relent in His judgment.

Even in regards to Lot, Abraham could have been less understanding than he was. He could have readily used one of the standby clichés we so often use, like 'he made his bed, now he's got to sleep in it,' but instead his heart broke for the righteous, and he began to plead with God. Abraham loved, therefore he interceded. Abraham loved, therefore he took the time to come before God, and agonize over individuals he didn't even know.

I doubt very much this was Abraham's first prayer on behalf of Lot, or even the righteous in Sodom, because when one loves, they persist in the love they possess without reservation or thought of giving up. A heart that loves is never disinterested, cold, distant, or unaffected by the plight or even judgment of others. A heart that loves is always interceding, it is always pleading with God for mercy and restoration.

Even when God gives a difficult message, even when He speaks judgment upon an individual or a nation, we cannot revel in this, but in our quiet time, in our prayer time, we must come before Him and do as Abraham did, interceding in love for those whom God has counted worthy of judgment. We must pray for repentance, we must pray for restoration, we must pray for grace and mercy, because that is what a loving heart does.

Yes, we preach the truth unashamedly, we proclaim that which God has commanded us to proclaim, but love still compels us to come before Him with supplication and petition, to stand in the gap and intercede. Love like Abraham and love will compel you to pray for the lost and the dying. Love like Abraham and you too will petition God to spare the righteous wherever, and however many they might be.

Abraham could have also bypassed God and gone directly to the people of Sodom, telling them to flee, and telling them judgment was coming. It is one thing when God tells you to go and warn a city or a nation, it's quite another to take it upon yourself to do so. Unless God gives you specific instruction to warn the people, the best course of action you can take is to bring your prayers of intercession before God. Pray for the nation you are in, pray for your neighbors, your family, your friends, long before you sermonize or try to evangelize them. It is God who stirs the heart to repentance, it is God who draws men unto Himself, and prayers on behalf of the lost are an essential link in the chain of an individual coming to Christ with true repentance of heart.

Because Abraham had a solid relationship with God, he also cared for his contemporaries and pleaded with God on their behalf. The love of God compels us to love our fellow man. The love of God compels us to intercede and come before Him not occasionally, or once in a while, but continually and with steadfastness. Abraham could have given up after his first petition. He could have shrugged his shoulders after throwing out the number fifty in regards to Sodom, and said, 'well, that's that. I did my part. It was worth a try.'

Instead of giving up however, Abraham tried again, and again, lessening the number, hoping against hope that God would spare the city for the sake of the righteous dwelling therein. From Abraham's conversation with God, we can also infer that sometimes God spares a city laden with sin, due to the handful of righteous living therein.

Genesis 18:26, "And the Lord said, 'If I find in Sodom fifty righteous within the city, then I will spare all the place for their sake.'"

For the sake of fifty righteous, God would have spared the entire place. Do you realize that the world is currently mocking, belittling, and defaming the very people, due to whom, the city they are in has not as yet been judged of God? Do you realize that for the sake of the righteous God is withholding His judgment for yet a little while longer? When we possess the heart of God, we can't help but weep on behalf of our people and our nation. Upon seeing Israel as it was, Jeremiah wept. Paul wept on behalf of his countrymen. Upon seeing Jerusalem as it was, Jesus wept. Upon seeing America as it is, we ought to likewise weep, petitioning God not for clemency, but for a little more time to reach the lost, to preach the gospel, and to lift high the name of Christ.

We cannot grow cold and callous; we cannot disengage, run to the hills, and never give those we have left behind a second thought, because our duty is not to be at ease in Zion but to be beacons of light that others might likewise find it. This is not a game of musical chairs. We ought not to be content merely because we have found a seat at the table, but love must compel us to cry out, and to reach out, even when those we are trying to reach misconstrue our intentions and despise us for it.

If before God judged Sodom the citizenry thereof would have heard that a man named Abraham was praying for them and interceding on their behalf, they likely would have laughed and mocked as enthusiastically as those of our day do upon hearing that someone is praying for them. We do not pray for the lost to get a thank you from them. We do not pray for the lost so they might appreciate us, or see how loving a Christian we really are. We pray for the lost because it is our duty, and the love of God burning in our hearts compels us.

Most of the time interceding on behalf of the lost is a thankless endeavor–one for which you will likely be mocked and ridiculed–but you do it nevertheless because it is your nature. You have been transformed, renewed, given a new heart, and your new heart beats for those who have not as yet come to know the love and mercy of Christ Jesus.

> *Romans 9:3-5, "For I could wish that I myself were accursed from Christ for my brethren, my kinsmen, according to the flesh, who are Israelites, to whom pertain the adoption, the glory, the covenants, the giving of the law, the service of God, and the promises; of whom are the fathers and from whom, according to the flesh, Christ came, who is over all, the eternally blessed God. Amen."*

Paul's singular, all-consuming desire was to see the salvation of his brethren, and his kinsmen…his fellow Israelites. Paul was not a man to mince words, and if he wrote that he could wish himself accursed from Christ for his brethren, it was not because he couldn't find the right words, and it was not as though he meant something else. This was his heart, this was his motivation, and this was his passion.

Is your passion for the lost on par with Paul's? If not, why not?

We must be motivated to go beyond our comfort level when attempting to reach the lost, not because of some earthly reward we might receive, but because of the eternal reward which is waiting for us. We attempt to reach the lost, not because at the end of the month we'll have more commitment cards to show off than the church across the street, but because the love of Jesus compels us to be tireless in our trumpeting His love and mercy toward mankind.

May we labor while we can, doing all we can for the Kingdom.

We know the future of the unrepentant sinner. We know the end result of those who continue to reside in the Sodom of sin, and refuse to come out of it. It is this knowledge that keeps us knocking at the door hoping to get an answer. We Christians have been called many names over the years, from hateful, to intolerant, to bigoted, but is it not more hateful to let someone walk into the flame without lifting a finger to keep them from it? Is it not more hateful to watch someone going to hell without warning them, pleading with them to turn around?

It is however the way of the enemy to redefine love and make it mean hate, to redefine concern and make it mean intolerance, to redefine truth and make it mean a lie. The tactics of the enemy are well known, and as wise children of God we ought to be privy to his schemes already, and as such be undeterred from our mission and purpose.

When discussing the prayer of Abraham, one can't help but notice the attitude with which he approached God. Men who truly know God approach Him with the requisite reverence. Men who only have a tangential relationship with God however, seem to lack reverence altogether. One cannot truly know God and not approach Him from a position of awe and amazement. One cannot truly know God and come before Him slothfully, or as though He was something less than what He is.

When we come before men of power or influence, we tend to do so, being on our best behavior and acting respectfully. With how much more respect, reverence and esteem ought we to approach the creator of all that is? No, it is not legalism, it is common sense. Although Abraham was God's friend, although he knew God on an intimate and profound level, He still approached God with reverence and veneration because of who He is.

Genesis 18:22, "Then the men turned away from there and went toward Sodom, but Abraham still stood before the Lord."

Abraham stood before the Lord, and he knew he was standing before the Lord. Even though Abraham was God's friend, he lived with the awareness of who God was, and acted accordingly. Abraham acknowledged the authority of God, he acknowledged the sovereignty of God, and he acknowledged that the One to whom he prayed was Lord over his life.

While it is true that God looks on the heart, and it is the heart He searches, and it is the heart He reads, often times our attitude toward God betrays the inner inconsistency of the heart. If our hearts are right before God, then our attitude toward God will mirror this inner truth. If our hearts are not right before God, then this will likewise be mirrored in our attitude toward Him. Our time of pray is a special experience. When we pray we are communicating and fellowshipping with God. This truth alone ought to stir within us the sentiment of reverence and respect.

Genesis 18:2-3, "So he lifted his eyes and looked, and behold, three men were standing by him; and when he saw them, he ran from the tent door to meet them, and bowed himself to the ground, and said, 'My Lord, if I have now found favor in Your sight, do not pass on by Your servant.'"

First off, Abraham recognized the three men as messengers of God. On the outside, they looked like regular men, seeing as this is the way the Bible describes them, but Abraham knew instinctively what the human eye could not perceive. The three men standing by Abraham were of supernatural origin, and Abraham knew this instantaneously. Even though he had a relationship with God the likes of which only a handful of individuals in the history of mankind enjoyed, Abraham did not take it for granted, or think he was entitled to special treatment because of it. He still bowed himself to the ground when he saw the three men, and referred to himself as God's servant.

Abraham was humble enough to bow himself to the ground before the messengers of the Lord. It was not the Lord Himself who stood before Abraham, it was His messengers, and yet Abraham still saw himself unworthy of meeting their gaze, or standing shoulder to shoulder with them. God gives grace to the humble. It is a known reality confirmed within the pages of Scripture. Abraham's attitude while encountering the messengers of the Lord and even when speaking to the Lord Himself was one of humility, and God honored this. Not only is a permissive, irreverent, nonchalant attitude accepted within the household of faith nowadays, it is promoted and encouraged.

If we truly realized who it was we were standing before, coming before God in prayer would never be a casual affair. With every utterance, with every petition, with every prayer prayed, we would exemplify reverence, and come before the mercy seat with humility and meekness of heart. Few things are more off-putting to God than pride, or a supposed servant coming before Him as though they were the master, and beginning to demand rather than petition.

Yes, I know, it is popular doctrine nowadays to demand of God, and act as though we are entitled, but show me one prayer in the Bible that was prayed from a position of entitlement and demand. There are no such prayers. Every true man of God, every true servant, knew to approach God with a spirit of reverence, and respect, and do so with humility of heart. They knew who it was they were standing before, and though God might have called individuals such as Abraham friend, not one abused this title, or took it for granted.

Yes, God is our Father, He is our Shepherd, He is our Healer, He is our Provider, He is our Savior, but He is also God, Master, King, and Lord. Be still, and know that He is God.

Another aspect of Abraham's attitude when communing with God that is worth noting is that he came near.

Genesis 18:23, "And Abraham came near and said, 'Would you also destroy the righteous with the wicked?'"

Prayer is the awareness that we are speaking to God, but it also necessitates coming near to Him. If prayer necessitates coming near to the Lord, then the next logical question is how ought our lives to be when we come near to the Lord?

Hebrews 10:19-22, "Therefore, brethren having boldness to enter the Holiest by the blood of Jesus, by a new and living way which He consecrated for us, through the veil, that is, His flesh, and having a High Priest over the house of God, let us draw near with a true heart in full assurance of faith, having our hearts sprinkled from an evil conscience and our bodies washed with pure water."

Through the blood of Jesus we have the boldness to enter the Holiest, yet it is incumbent upon us as individuals to draw near with a true heart, having our hearts sprinkled from an evil conscience and our bodies washed with pure water. In Christ, through Christ, and His shed blood we have access to the Holiest, because He consecrated this new and living way for us, but this does not mean that we are without responsibility when it comes to approaching God effectively. When our hearts are true, when they have been sprinkled from an evil conscience, and our bodies have been washed with pure water, then we can draw near in full assurance of faith, because we know Jesus made a way for us, being the High Priest over the house of God.

Man does not like conditions and stipulations, but they exist nonetheless. Yes, there are conditions and stipulations to effective prayer, and one of these conditions is that our hearts be sprinkled from an evil conscience, and our bodies washed with pure water. Did I come up with these stipulations? No, it was the Word of God, so it is the Word we must contend with if we desire to change or twist what has been written. There is so much that must be set aright within the household of faith before we can hope to have a dynamic, powerful, and ongoing relationship with God, that we have not a minute to waste.

It all begins with whether or not we are willing to surrender, disavow, and do away with our preconceived notions, pet doctrines, hidden sins, and other stumbling blocks hindering the lines of communication between ourselves and God. Are we willing to humble ourselves, are we willing to approach God as servants even though He might see us as friends? Are we willing to lay aside the foolish notion that we can somehow dictate terms to God, or as little gods create our own reality?

Abraham was a man to whom the messengers of the Lord came, with whom the messengers of the Lord dined, and to whom

God Himself spoke. Yet Abraham still sees himself as nothing more than dust and ashes.

Genesis 18:27, "Then Abraham answered and said, 'Indeed now, I who am but dust and ashes have taken it upon myself to speak to the Lord.'"

I have heard so many flippant prayers throughout my life, prayers prayed by men with diplomas and degrees, graduates of prestigious seminaries, who didn't seem to grasp the basic and fundamental essence that prayer first and foremost must be a humbling of oneself, and a glorifying of God. We don't pray to accentuate our own self-worth, we don't pray to highlight our own accomplishments, we don't pray to remind God how good and noble and righteous and holy we are. We pray to commune and fellowship with the Father, creator of all, and ruler of all.

There was no arrogance in Abraham as he approached God. There was no sense of entitlement, there was no glorying in his good works…there was a humbling of oneself long before Abraham asked anything of God. Before Abraham petitioned God, and interceded on behalf of Sodom, he humbled himself, and bowed himself to the ground before the messengers of the Lord. Pride and arrogance impede our prayers. They are as lead weights tethered to our words, keeping them from ascending to the heavens.

Job 35:12-13, "There they cry out, but He does not answer, because of the pride of evil men. Surely God will not listen to empty talk, nor will the Almighty regard it."

God does not listen to the empty talk of prideful and evil men. He does not even regard their prayers, or their words, nor will He answer when they cry out. Abraham lived a life of self-renunciation, and self-denial. It is next to impossible to still be prideful, boastful, arrogant, and haughty when you are standing before the Almighty, He who knows your heart, your innermost thoughts, and the intent with which you performed every task He has ever assigned you.

It is because men do not know the one true God that they are still able to pray from a position of arrogance and pride. It is because they have never beheld Him in all His glory, nor understood the nature of Him, that they are able to pray from a position of entitlement. Once we come to know God as Abraham did, we also come to know that we are not entitled to absolutely anything in this life. An entitlement is a right to benefits specified by law or contract. Although God freely gives us salvation, as well as sonship, it does not mean we are, or ever were entitled to these things. What it does mean, is that the grace and mercy of God were such that He chose to adopt us, and make us His own. If anything, this is reason to give glory and praise to God, not to walk about as tough we accomplished something in and of ourselves.

It also took boldness on the part of Abraham to approach God, to come near to Him, and speak to Him. No, nothing in life is as simple as it first appears. Within Abraham's coming near to the Lord, and his speaking to him, we see an amalgam of virtues, all playing off each other, all intertwined and interconnected, like a beautiful symphony of the soul. You can't fake Abraham's heart. You can't fake humbling oneself, while sprinkling one's heart from an evil conscience, while coming near to the Lord, while maintaining the requisite reverence.

There are just too many aspects one must be aware of for this to have been anything other than a truly righteous man, who was truly humble, who truly knew God, and who truly revered Him. There is an unbridgeable gap between pretending to be, and actually being. Today many Christians are playing the pretend game wherein they affix a date in their mind as to when they believe Jesus will come, and try their hardest to be good people until that date arrives. Every few months the date gets moved up, and people once more try to hold their breaths, and be on their best behavior, hoping Jesus finds them as righteous as humanly possible.

And here is where we trip up. We try to be as righteous as humanly possible, when to God our righteousness is as filthy rags.

When we humble ourselves, when we see ourselves as dust and ashes, and acknowledge that it is only by the righteousness of Christ and His shed blood that God sees us as righteous, then we will strive not to live up to some denominational notion of righteousness, but simply to be more like Jesus, the embodiment of righteousness. Abraham did not have boldness because of who he was, but because of who God was. The only reason Abraham had the confidence he had, was because his heart did not condemn him, and because his heart did not condemn him, he knew he could approach God.

1 John 3:21-22, "Beloved, if our heart does not condemn us, we have confidence toward God. And whatever we ask we receive from Him, because we keep His commandments and do those things that are pleasing in His sight."

The instant your heart condemns you of something, you lose all confidence in regards to approaching God. Whether it's an argument you had with your spouse that was not resolved, a word of gossip you passed on to fellow brothers or sisters, it doesn't have to be some big, overwhelming thing…just enough for your heart to condemn you. When this occurs, the first and only course of action is repentance. Repent of the gossip, repent of the argument, set it right, and then come before the Lord, and you will see that once repentance has taken place, you can approach Him with confidence.

Hebrews 4:16, "Let us therefore come boldly to the throne of grace, that we may obtain mercy and find grace to help in time of need."

If our hearts condemn us, then we have no confidence toward God, and if we have no confidence toward God, we cannot come boldly to the throne of grace. Because we cannot come boldly to the throne of grace, we can neither obtain mercy, nor find grace to help in time of need. And it all starts with lack of confidence due to something our heart condemns us of. One of the more obvious characteristics of Abraham and his prayer is his persistence. Just because it's obvious however, it does not mean it ought not to be mentioned or discussed.

If we could use only one word to describe Abraham, what is the one word that would come to mind? Humble, obedient, faithful, are all words that would readily spring up when considering Abraham, but so would persistent. In his prayer of intercession for Sodom and the righteous therein, Abraham was nothing if not persistent.

Abraham begins his intercession in regards to Sodom at fifty righteous souls. Perhaps it was due to all that he had heard concerning Sodom, or his awareness of how few righteous there were, but no longer feeling comfortable with the number fifty, Abraham comes before God again and lowers the bar to forty-five.

This goes on for some time, from forty-five, to forty, to thirty, to twenty, and eventually to ten righteous souls in the whole of Sodom. Abraham essentially bargained with God, for the lives of the citizenry of Sodom, and if there had been ten righteous souls in Sodom, as per His Word, God would have spared it. From reading the Word of God, we know that ten was still too high a number, but the fact that Abraham interceded on their behalf, gave Sodom a chance to be saved, it gave them one final opportunity to be spared.

The pessimist in us might be quick to roll our eyes, and think to ourselves, 'his prayer and intercession didn't do anyone any good anyway since Sodom still got destroyed,' but what we cannot fail to acknowledge is that destruction came because sin was so rampant that not even ten righteous were found within the walls of the city, and not because Abraham somehow failed in his intercession.

Sometimes we will intercede on behalf of an individual, or even a nation and God's judgment still comes. This does not, in any way, mean that our intercession has failed, or that we ought to stop interceding on behalf of those we are interceding for. What it does mean, is that although God afforded the individual or the nation another opportunity for repentance, they rejected it as they had all the previous times God attempted to reach out to them in love.

Our duty is to pray. Our duty is to intercede. Our duty is to be persistent in our petitions for those who are still lost, and God in His sovereign wisdom will do as He must. As long as you live, and as long as the sinner for which you are praying still breathes and has not come to stand before the judgment seat of Christ, keep praying, and keep interceding. There is still hope.

The Word of God teaches us that Abraham stood in the gap; he interceded for Sodom though Sodom did not know anyone was interceding on their behalf. A prayer of intercession, whether for an individual or a nation, is essentially standing in the gap, standing in the breach, and pleading with God to relent from His predetermined judgments.

Psalm 106:23, "Therefore He said that He would destroy them, had not Moses His chosen one stood before Him in the breach, to turn away His wrath, lest He destroy them."

This is an instance when intercession bore fruit. Moses interceded on behalf of Israel, whom God, in His wrath, had purposed to destroy, and because he stood in the breach, God turned away His wrath and did not destroy them. It took one man to save a nation from destruction. It took one true servant such as Moses, to stand in the breach and plead on behalf of the people of Israel, and God relented, and His wrath was turned away because one man prayed.

If you've ever wanted to know the true power of prayer, this is it!

One man prayed, and the wrath of God was turned away. One man prayed, and an entire nation was spared destruction.

Jeremiah 18:19-20, "Give heed to me, O Lord, and listen to the voice of those who contend with me! Shall evil be repaid for good? For they have dug a pit for my life. Remember that I stood before You to speak good for them, and to turn away Your wrath from them."

We find Jeremiah praying to God, reminding Him of his intercession on behalf of the selfsame people who were contending with him, and who had dug a pit for his life. Jeremiah had prayed for his people, he had stood before God and spoke well of them, that God's wrath might be turned away, and the people repaid him by trying to take his life.

Yes, often times good is repaid with evil, and those for which we pray despise us all the more earnestly. Yes, often times the only recompense for having spent hours on end in prayer on behalf of someone will be their disdain, but God remembers our prayers, He sees our hearts, and gives to each one according to their works. We cannot grow cold, disheartened, or indifferent just because those for which we are praying are persecuting us or treating us as though we were a reproach to them. When the day comes that they see the light, receive truth, and are transformed by the grace of Christ, those selfsame individuals who are now defaming and denigrating you, will thank God for your prayers, and thank you for never giving up on them.

Even so, it is not about the thanks you might one day receive from those for whom you interceded, it is about the fact that God seeks a man who will stand in the gap before Him on behalf of the land.

Ezekiel 22:30, "So I sought for a man among them who would make a wall, and stand in the gap before Me on behalf of the land, that I should not destroy it; but I found no one."

To this day God is looking for intercessors. He is looking for those who would consider others before themselves, and pray on behalf of others instead of praying for themselves. God honors such hearts, and lends His ear to their pleas. God is looking for one who would intercede, who would make a wall, and stand in the gap, and pray for the land that God would not destroy it. Will He find someone, or will it be as it was?

Ezekiel 33:7-8, "So you, son of man: I have made you a watchman for the house of Israel; therefore you shall hear a word from My mouth and warn them for Me. When I say to the wicked, 'O wicked man, you shall surely die!' and you do not speak to warn the wicked from his way, that wicked man shall die in his iniquity; but his blood I will require at your hand."

If we who know the love of God, the grace of God, the mercy of God, and the heart of God will not intercede, stand in the gap and make a wall, who will? Abraham interceded on behalf of the vilest city of his time, and asked that God spare it due to the handful of righteous souls therein. Warn the wicked…it is your duty. Warn the wicked that their blood might be required of your hand. Abraham did his duty before God, and God blessed him for it. Abraham prayed, he interceded, he petitioned God repeatedly and persistently, and God gave in to his petitions time and again.

Have we done all we can to intercede on behalf of the lost? Have we petitioned God ardently and fervently on behalf of those we might not even know, except that they need salvation? These are questions only we can answer upon searching our hearts diligently. We behold the men and women of the Bible, we see their lives of prayer and humility, and we realize that they were human just as we are human, and yet they were able to have the ear of God, and through their prayers compel God to withhold His wrath and relent in judging.

God has not changed, and His heart is still tender toward the intercessors among us. God still sees, God still hears, and God still answers. May we intercede as Abraham interceded so we may know the presence and power of God as Abraham did!

CHAPTER TWO
THE PRAYER OF JACOB

The history of Jacob has always been fascinating to me. Not only was he one of the patriarchs of the Hebrew nation, he was also a man of prayer. Every one of us, at one time or another has seen a little of themselves in Jacob. He was by no means a perfect man, but he was a man who understood the importance of a relationship with God. We often find Jacob on the mountaintop, or down in the valley. We either find him reveling in victory, or wallowing in defeat.

Although the life of Jacob is often times controversial–since stealing birthrights was not a common occurrence in his day–it is nevertheless a life worthy of study and examination. This being an exploration of prayer however, we will table our discussion on the particulars of Jacob's life, and focus exclusively on discussing his prayer life, and the intimacy he shared with God.

Genesis 32:9-12, "Then Jacob said, 'O God of my father Abraham and God of my father Isaac, the Lord who said to me, 'Return to your country and to your kindred, and I will deal well with you': I am not worthy of the least of all the mercies and of all the truth which You have shown Your servant; for I crossed over this Jordan with my staff, and now I have become two companies. Deliver me, I pray, from the hand of my brother, from the hand of Esau; for I fear him, lest he come and attack me and the mother with the children. For You said, 'I will surely treat you well, and make your descendants as the sand of the sea, which cannot be numbered for multitude.'"

Although the Bible tells us of other prayers Jacob prayed, this is the most telling of all when it comes to just how well Jacob knew God. Jacob had no Bible, and still he knew God. He had no temple, no house of worship, no altar, and still he prayed to God. He has no clear doctrine, no confession of faith as we do today, no

Sunday school, no church to attend, no synagogue to worship in, and still he lived a life of prayer.

In his personal life, especially within the context of relationship with his own family, Jacob is a deceiver, and is in turn deceived because what a man sows is what a man reaps. He trusts men, and is summarily disappointed. He sins against his brother Esau, fleeing his home for fear of his brother, is compelled to repent of what he did, and after twenty years of exile finally returns to his homeland.

Twenty years is a long time for anyone, especially so for someone who is homesick and desires to see the place of his birth again. I came to America when I was nine years old. It was six years before I, or any member of my family, could legally return to Romania without running the risk of being imprisoned or worse. For those six years, every once in a while I would listen to my mother and father, or my grandmother and my grandfather reminisce about our homeland, and every time, they did so with pathos and a sense of longing. No matter how far we stray from our homeland, there is still a part of us that yearns to see it once more, to return and feel the soil between our toes and breathe in the air we remember when we were young and life was carefree.

Jacob had left with only his staff, crossing the Jordan and fleeing from before the wrath of his brother, and now he was returning, a wealthy man in his own right. Still, he remembered what had been, the bitterness and hatred between himself and his brother Esau, and now Jacob stood before God in prayer. The boy who left, now returned a man, seasoned and matured in the ways of life, and even treachery by none other than his father-in-law Laban.

It was Laban who taught Jacob what would later come to be known as the bait-and-switch. It was Laban who tricked Jacob into serving him twice as long as he first agreed to, and all these things were as worthwhile lessons for Jacob. The lessons of life mature us and grow us. No matter how hurtful, troubling, uncomfortable, or seemingly unfair, it is the lessons of life that chisel away the unnecessary and mold us into something new.

As is always the case, the hand which holds the chisel is responsible for the finished product, and not the chisel itself. If life's lessons are the chisel, then we must assume that He who is holding the chisel knows exactly what He desires the end result to be. The chisels in life are a means to a glorious end. Some of us need more chiseling than others, but however much the Master must cut away, it will all be worth it in the end.

In order to understand the reason for Jacob's prayer, and the fervency thereof, we must contextualize what it was he was feeling at this particular moment. Jacob knew full well that his brother Esau had sworn that once their father breathed his last, Esau would see him dead. Jacob knew the reason he fled his home and everything he'd ever known, and it wasn't because he didn't like the dry climate, or his mother's dessert choice after dinner. Jacob had tricked his brother Esau into selling him his birthright, and then tricked their father by pretending to be Esau and receiving the blessing.

Jacob knew exactly why Esau hated him, and he knew it was not unwarranted by any means. After twenty years, Jacob still feared his brother, knowing what he had done, yet because God had told him to return to his country, he overcame his fear and obeyed.

The life of Jacob teaches us that no one can outrun their sin. Eventually, your sin will catch up with you, and the consequences thereof will be as an impenetrable barrier. Sin must be dealt with in our lives. Sin must be repented of, that it might be forgiven and that we might walk in assurance of faith. It had been twenty years, and the sin of Jacob still weighed heavily upon him. Twenty years had gone by, and still Jacob feared the wrath of his brother Esau for what he had done, because he had never repented of his deed to his brother. He had never owned up to what he had done, he had just fled.

Numbers 32:23, "But if you do not do so, then take note, you have sinned against the Lord; and be sure your sin will find you out."

This is one of those universal truths which many people have a hard time grasping. No matter how well you hide your sin from your spouse, from your family, from your friends, it will, inevitably, invariably, eventually find you out. From famous preachers, to prominent pastors, to laymen, if they have chosen the way of sin, and rather than repent of it they simply hide it, eventually it boils over, floats to the surface, and thoroughly shames them.

Because Jacob never dealt with the deception he perpetrated on his father and brother, because he never confronted the issue but simply ran from it, twenty years later it was still a burden, and something he finally had to deal with. Sin festers. It is not a docile thing that bears no consequence or burden. It grows and consumes and metastasizes, because by its very nature it is a destructive force. Sin destroys. Sin consumes. Sin evolves, drawing its victims deeper and deeper into the darkness and mire of destructive practice.

There is no such thing as a little sin. What we might deem as a little sin, will invariably lead us to bigger ones, and if we do not uproot it from our hearts at inception, we will eventually find ourselves far from God and His light. It is the way sin works, and those who have played with sin, and flirted with it, and allowed themselves certain liberties thinking they were innocent frivolities and nothing more, have come to know just how beguiling sin can be, and what it can lead to.

Although it is not known who informed Esau of Jacob's imminent return from Mesopotamia, what is known is that Jacob's sin had finally found him out, it had finally caught up with him, and now he was terrified of having to see his brother face to face after all these years.

Genesis 32:6, "Then the messengers returned to Jacob, saying, 'We came to your brother Esau, and he also is coming to meet you, and four hundred men are with him.'"

Knowing what he knew about how he'd left things with his brother, upon hearing that Esau was coming to meet him with four hundred men, Jacob likely concluded one thing: Esau was coming to take his revenge, and he was bringing an army with him.

Genesis 32:7, "So Jacob was greatly afraid and distressed; and he divided his people that were with him, and the flocks and herds and camels, into two companies."

Hearing that the brother who wanted you dead for stealing his birthright is coming to meet you with an army of four hundred men would put a crimp in anyone's day. Jacob was greatly afraid and distressed, and rightly so, remembering what he had done, and how deceitful he had been toward his brother Esau.

Within this verse we also see something admirable in Jacob, something few in his position would have had the wherewithal to do. Jacob takes action immediately. He does not wallow in his fear, nor does he wallow in his distress. He sets about planning for his brother's arrival, and divides his people, his flocks, and his camels into two companies. Granted, what he did seems insignificant, seeing as four hundred men were approaching him with his brother Esau at the forefront, but the fact that Jacob was not paralyzed by his fear is something we must take into account, and attempt to emulate.

Genesis 32:8, "And he said, 'If Esau comes to the one company and attacks it, then the other company which is left will escape.'"

Here was Jacob, doing all that was in his power to do, and preparing for the worst possible outcome. After all his preparations however, after dividing his people into two companies, and hoping that one could escape if the other was attacked, Jacob also realized how limited his preparations were. He realized that what he had been able to do was ineffective and of very little value, so he proceeded to do something more, something that was not dependent on his prowess, his cunning, or his strength. Jacob proceeded to pray.

It is human nature to strategize and come up with contingency plans when we see danger approaching. When we come to the point of panic, when we become greatly afraid and distressed, we will grasp at any straw, reach out for any semblance of a lifeline, and try our utmost to save ourselves. Eventually, given enough time, we realize the true measure of our impotence. We realize we cannot save ourselves, and so we go before the One we know is able to save us, and keep us and protect us. After trying to do it all on our own, eventually we run to God, but it would be far wiser still to run to God in the first place, and bypass the fear, and the distress, bypass the feeling of impotence and powerlessness, and just trust in the mighty hand of our God, who is mighty to save.

Admirable as Jacob's prayer might be, it would have been far more admirable if he had run to prayer first.

Even the best of us often times take it upon ourselves to spare ourselves or save ourselves in certain situations. The flesh revels in the notion that we can affect change, or that we are somehow captains of our own ships, masters of our own destinies, and determiners of our own fate. Manmade plans fail because they are made by men. No matter how well we plan for every possible contingency, you can't plan for everything, because our minds are not infinite as the mind of God is. We can see certain angles, foresee certain hardships, but we can't see all the angles or all the hardships, and this is why we must trust in God. God sees it all, from beginning to end, and everything in between.

More importantly God knows the why of it all, from why certain trials are allowed to come over us, to why we are told to stay in a certain place while others are being told to flee. God does not have a collective plan for His children. He is an intimate and individual God, and our place of refuge and safety is in His will, and nowhere else. Around the fire, or through the fire, wherever God leads us, He will protect us, and we must do as Jacob did, and stand on His promise. We must overcome our fears, our reservations, our predisposition to thinking we know better than God, or that we can come up with a better plan, and obey Him. Go when He tells you to go, stay when He tells you to stay, and pray always, for it is the means by which we communicate with Him.

It took Jacob twenty years, a handful of heartaches, countless hardships, and numerous disappointments, but he is finally on the right path, humble enough to go before God with prayer and supplication and ask for His help. So what was so special about Jacob's prayer, and why is it worth discussing at this juncture?

First of all, Jacob's prayer was the prayer of a man who knew God only partially. No, we can never know God in His fullness, but we can continually grow in the knowledge of Him. Growing in God is a natural and mandatory part of our relationship with Him. So how did I come to the conclusion that Jacob knew God partially? I came to this conclusion by meditating on his prayer, and the phraseology thereof.

Jacob begins his prayer with the following words: 'O God of my father Abraham and God of my father Isaac.' Although Jacob acknowledged God, and prayed to Him, he referred to God as the God of his father Abraham and Isaac. As yet, God was not personal to Jacob. He knew God only as the God of his forefathers, but not as Lord and King of his life. As yet Jacob does not have the boldness to say 'my God,' but instead refers to Him as the God of his forefathers.

This is relevant, because although thousands of years have passed since Jacob's prayer, many still walk about thinking of God as the God of those who came before them, and not their own personal God. Many a soul adopts a certain denomination because their parents or their grandparents grew up in it, and they filter their faith through the prism of their forefathers' faith. Even though God had spoken to Jacob, he still thought of Him as being the God of his fathers.

Jacob even goes so far as to acknowledge the sovereignty of God, the omnipotence of God, but he does not personalize his reference to the Lordship of God. He does not say 'my Lord,' but rather 'the Lord.' 'But that's just semantics isn't it? You're just grasping at straws…does it really matter?' Yes, it matters. It really matters. Whether or not God is personal to you, whether He is your God or the God of your fathers matters a great deal.

John 20:26-28, "And after eight days His disciples were again inside, and Thomas with them. Jesus came, the doors being shut, and stood in the midst, and said, 'Peace to you!' Then He said to Thomas, 'Reach your finger here, and look at My hands; and reach your hand here, and put it into My side. Do not be unbelieving, but believing.' And Thomas answered and said to Him, 'My Lord and my God!'"

We see the marked difference between the wording of Jacob's prayer, and Thomas' reaction at seeing Jesus and touching Him. Thomas did not say, 'God of my father,' instead he made it personal and intimate by saying, 'my Lord and my God!' Know the God before whom you stand, not as some secondhand God, but as a personal God, one who knows you better than you know yourself, one who hears your prayers and petitions, and one who loves and cares for you.

In reading the history of Jacob we come to realize that God always looked out for him. God even revealed Himself to Jacob when he was fleeing the wrath of his brother Esau, going so far as to show him a ladder leading to heaven in a dream. God attempted, and repeatedly so, to reach out to Jacob and establish a relationship with him.

Even with the promise that God would be with him, even with seeing an army of angels as he approached his homeland, Jacob still felt fearful and dreaded meeting up with his brother Esau. Even with all that God shows us on a daily basis, even with all the ways He reveals Himself to us continually, we, as Jacob, often doubt, grow fearful and despondent concerning things over which we have no control to begin with. We can take our fears, our doubts, our apprehensions, and our concerns to God in prayer and see Him work them out in a way only He can, or we can trust in our own wisdom and abilities and carry these burdens on our own. The choice is ours to make.

When we come to know God personally, and view Him as our Lord and our God, the fears melt away, and we learn to trust He who is able to carry us through our trials and hardships. The only reason men doubt God is because they don't know Him well enough. If they truly knew God, then they would never doubt any of His promises, or His ability to save and preserve His beloved. Grow in the knowledge of God, and you will know perfect peace, joy, and safety.

Because Jacob did not know God as he ought to have, even though God had reached out to him repeatedly, he was fearful of his brother, and distressed at the prospect of having to look him in the eyes after twenty years.

Know God. Don't be content with hearing about Him from a preacher, a friend, or even myself; know Him personally, and intimately and passionately. If you seek Him, you will find Him. God is not hiding from His children. God is waiting for His children to pursue Him, and with every step we take toward Him, He will take two steps toward us. It is presupposed that every individual who prays to God, must know God. This is a misguided supposition. Some pray to God without ever knowing Him.

> *Acts 17:22-24, "Then Paul stood in the midst of the Areopagus and said, 'Men of Athens, I perceive that in all things you are very religious; for as I was passing through and considering the objects of your worship, I even found an altar with this inscription: TO THE UNKNOWN GOD. Therefore, the One whom you worship without knowing, Him I proclaim to you: God, who made the world and everything in it, since He is Lord of heaven and earth, does not dwell in temples made with hands.'"*

By Paul's own words, the Athenians were worshipping God, without knowing Him. To know God, is to love God, and to love God is to die to self and all that it entails. It is as it was, and many today worship God without really knowing Him. Even though Jacob did not know God as he ought, even though he does not have the wherewithal to call Him his God, Jacob prays with humility and reverence. 'I am not worthy of the least of all the mercies and of all the truth which You have shown Your servant.'

Not only do we see reverence and humility in the prayer of Jacob, we also see him begin to identify himself as a servant of God. Even within the short time frame that it took Jacob to pray this prayer, we are starting to see a certain level of maturing taking place. There is nothing that matures a man faster than hardship, and Jacob found himself in the midst of a world of hardship. Realizing none of his plans would suffice if his brother Esau decided to attack him with his four hundred men, Jacob comes before God, and begins to pray a prayer that the self-assured and borderline haughty Jacob of twenty years past would have never prayed.

Jacob sees himself as undeserving, and unworthy of the least of all the mercies God had shown him over the years, realizing also that these blessings, these mercies, were not created or brought about by his hand, but by the hand of God. Do we acknowledge the blessings of God and identify them as such? Do we look at the mercies God has shown us and thank Him for them?

Jacob knew that all his hard work, all his strategizing, all his plans, would have amounted to little more than nothing if God had not blessed him and extended mercy toward him. Even though Jacob had but a rudimentary knowledge of God, he still knew enough to know that he ought to be thankful toward the God from whom all blessings come, and that indeed, they come from Him.

Another thing we would be wise to learn from the prayer of Jacob, is that the mercies God shows us are undeserved and unmerited. God does not bless us because we are better than our fellow brothers and sisters in Christ. God does not show us mercy or favor because we are better Christians, more righteous, or holier than the rest of the Body of Christ. He shows us all mercy in the way He chooses, and the way which is pleasing to Him. Since God is sovereign, He can do that, and all we can do is thank Him for the underserved mercies He showers upon us each and every day.

True men of God, who come to know Him intimately, come to realize just how generous God truly is. With each new mercy, with each new blessing, men of God become all the more aware that these mercies and blessings are undeserved and unmerited.

1 Corinthians 4:7, "For who makes you differ from another? And what do you have that you did not receive? Now if you did indeed receive it, why do you glory as if you had not received it?"

There is nothing that a man can possess which he did not receive. This is the essence of Paul's argument to the church at Corinth. Whether a spiritual gift, a material blessing, or a divine mercy, all things come from the hand of God, all things are received, and if all things are received of God, then we have no reason to glory in them as though we did not receive them. How can I be prideful of something if I know it isn't mine? How can I boast and glory in something if I know it was a gift, received from the hand of God, not because I deserved it, but just because He is so good?

I cannot for the life of me understand individuals whom God endows with a certain spiritual gift, who then turn around and expect their fellow brothers in Christ to raise them up and praise them as though they themselves were something special and unique. They take up titles for themselves, expect to be called by these titles, feel entitled to a life of ease and comfort, and expect brothers and sisters in Christ to obey them without question, all because they received something from God which was not their own, which they cannot claim or appropriate for themselves.

An individual who is able to grasp that all things come from the hand of God, and that they have nothing which they did not receive, is well on their way to understanding the deeper mysteries of man's relationship with God.

Although God blessed Jacob, and did so abundantly, he comes to the realization that he is unworthy of the many blessings of God. There are certain individuals, and I've run across a few of them myself, who begin to look down their noses on others when God begins to bless them. They begin to feel superior, or somehow more spiritual than their fellow believers, because they equate material blessing with God preferring them over those whom He did not bless as He blessed them. True servants know to humble themselves before God with each new blessing and each new mercy shown them, rather than allow pride or a sense of self-accomplishment to take root in their heart.

When we walk in humility, when we acknowledge we are undeserving of God's mercies as Jacob acknowledged, we leave no room for pride. The oxygen pride needs in order to breathe is effectively removed from our hearts as we walk in humility, and pride is choked off and expires because it has nothing to feed off of.

Lest we think Jacob's wealth was something to scoff at, or easily dismiss, we must keep in mind that the richest people of the time were those who possessed animals, whether goats, cows, donkeys or camels. Jacob lived in an agrarian culture, and one can only begin to imagine his wealth when understanding what he intended to give as a present to Esau his brother.

Genesis 32:13-15, "So he lodged there that same night, and took what came to his hand as a present for Esau his brother: two hundred female goats and twenty male goats, two hundred ewes and twenty rams, thirty milk camels and their colts, forty cows and ten bulls, twenty female donkeys and ten foals."

Due to the culture we live in, very few would look at a farmer or a rancher and consider them as wealthy or well off. We tend to see the glitzier careers, such as sports stars, or famous singers, but the only other man besides the president who was able to purchase a helicopter during the Communist regime in Romania, was none other than a sheep herder who had over twenty thousand sheep. No one else could afford the price, or the taxes on something so extravagant, except for a man who tended his sheep, made his cheese, and sold his wool every year.

Make no mistake, Jacob was a wealthy man by any standard, yet he beholds all that he has amassed, and after acknowledging they are all from the hand of God, he concludes that they are undeserved. Jacob took what came to his hand as a present to Esau, and his present was nothing to scoff at. To give away such things on a whim just because they come to your hand, you know you won't miss them and you have a lot more where those came from.

Obedience is not reserved only for the poor, it is not mandated only for those who have nothing by way of the material, but when God speaks, obedience is mandated of everyone. Jacob was a rich man. He could have pretended he did not hear the voice of God telling him to return to his homeland and face his brother, but he knew better, even with the limited understanding he possessed concerning God. Jacob knew he was dependent on God. How many supposed believers know this important truth?

Blessing can either make you humble, and thankful and grateful to God, or it can make you proud and arrogant and forgetful of God. The heart of man is the battlefield, and man's soul is the prize. It is within the heart that a battle rages between the self, and the Spirit of God. It is within the heart that two opposing forces clash and collide, and depending on which will have ultimate victory, we will either seek God all the more in our prosperity, or forget Him altogether.

As the old proverb so aptly states, if you put two dogs in a cage, the one you feed will ultimately win. Feed your spiritual man. Humble yourself in the sight of the Lord, and He will lift you up.

Another aspect of Jacob's prayer worthy of highlighting is that Jacob had a specific purpose to his prayer. There was nothing general about Jacob's prayer, there was nothing ambiguous or veiled.

'Deliver me, I pray, from the hand of my brother, from the hand of Esau; for I fear him, lest he come and attack me and the mother with the children.'

That is a pretty direct prayer. Jacob knew exactly what he needed from God, and he minced no words in his prayers. The only thing Jacob could have said that would have been more concise is, 'Lord help me! I fear Esau will kill me if You don't.'

Even when the purpose and goal of your prayer is birthed out of fear as Jacob's was, it is good to have a purpose when we pray. There are prayers of fellowship, wherein we commune with God, and speak to Him as to a loving Father, and then there are prayers of petition wherein we know exactly what it is we need, and focus on that particular thing. Jacob was petitioning God for protection, asking God to save him from the hand of his brother Esau, because he feared him. That's pretty specific, by any standard.

Jacob sees the danger, he sees he is helpless, he sees he has no one left to turn to, and he turns to God. His prayer is one of specificity, and purpose, one that does not suffer from a long introduction or an interlude. Jacob gets to the point, and he does so with urgency because he realizes the predicament he is in. There is not a shadow of the pride or arrogance from twenty years ago—it has all been stripped and burned from him—and now humbly, meekly, he petitions God to intervene on his behalf.

Jacob is not afraid to admit that he's afraid. There is no shame or reticence in Jacob's prayer. He opens his heart to God, and reveals his innermost being, testifying of the fear he possesses in regards to his brother Esau. I have known brothers in the Lord who thought it beneath them to admit they were afraid. They thought it something shameful or unbecoming to come before God and admit fear. Jacob, one of three Patriarchs, the spiritual and physical ancestors of Judaism, admitted to fear, he confessed it, and asked God for help in overcoming it.

We all have our fears. Whether we fear for our families, for our children, for our lives, for our health, whatever it is we fear for, we must confess before God, that He might intervene and deal with the root cause of our fear.

Yes, perfect love casts out fear, but in order for the fear to be cast out, it must be confessed that the perfect love of God might come in and do away with it. Jacob didn't just fear for himself, he feared for the mother and the children as well. It is in the small things that we can more readily gauge change in an individual. Man can pretty well fake his way through the big things, but when it comes to the details, to the nuances, that is when you begin to see the true nature of a man.

Jacob the selfish, Jacob the proud, Jacob the deceiver, fears for someone else other than himself. He fears for the mother and the children. It is in this instant that we know Jacob has had a true change of heart, that he is not the man he was twenty years prior. He becomes selfless, and puts the lives and needs of others ahead of his own. Yes, Jacob feared for himself as any man in his position would, for Esau had sworn vengeance, but he also remembers the mother and the children, fearing for them as well.

With all the emotions coursing through him, with all the fear, with all the doubt, with all the distress, Jacob still stood on the promises of God. No matter the fear he felt, Jacob would not be moved from the promises God had made to him, and he reminds God of these promises in his prayer.

Genesis 32:12, "For You said, 'I will surely treat you well, and make your descendants as the sand of the sea, which cannot be numbered for multitude.'"

Not only was Jacob aware of what God had promised him, he trusted in the promises of God. If we, as believers, as children of God and bondservants of Christ, would stand on the promises God has made to us, we would never again be anxious, fearful, or distressed. If we not only acknowledged the existence of these promises but believed them with all our heart, we would live with the awareness that not a hair upon our head will come to harm, because He who created all things and in whom are all things, is the keeper of our souls.

The Lord is our protector. He is faithful, and He keeps His promises. The Lord promised he would make Jacob's descendants as the sand of the sea, and Jacob reminded Him of that promise. At this juncture Jacob had no idea how this would come about, how his life would be spared from the wrath of his brother Esau, but he believed that God was able to fulfill His promise.

There is no denying the splash of doubt in Jacob's actions. There is no denying that he attempted to save himself before going to God, but now that he stood before God, he remembered all God promised him and began to draw strength. Not only can we learn practical lessons of what to do from the life and prayer of Jacob, we can also learn what not to do in certain instances, and learning from the mistakes of those who came before us will spare us much heartache in the long run.

As much as we would like to deny it, or pretend it isn't so, doubt is a constant companion on this journey of life. We doubt our own abilities, we doubt a certain endeavor will succeed, we doubt forfeiting food that actually tastes good for seaweed smoothies actually does have health benefits, but it is our duty as wise men and women of God to overcome doubt. Doubt is like a shroud that blurs everything around us. We do not see reality as we ought because doubt affects our perception. Neither do we see God as we should, because we are focusing on the doubt rather than on Him.

Doubt is the poison tipped arrow that does nothing more than breaks the skin…at first we think it inconsequential and irrelevant, we wave it off and ignore it, until it starts to get infected, we start to lose feeling in the area where the arrow nicked us, and before we know what happened we are returned to the earth from which we came.

In our moments of doubt we also try to help God, or somehow aid Him in answering our prayers faster, or in a way more acceptable to us. God knows what He's doing, and He asks that we trust He knows what He is doing. One of the most frustrating things we can do is second guess God all the time. It is frustrating both for ourselves and for Him, because each time we think we know better than God we end up running aground, and God has to delay His plan for our lives because we've chosen to take a circuitous route.

With your human reason, and with your eyes of flesh, you might see green pastures and wildflowers, but God sees beyond the meadow to the cliff just out of sight. Trust that God has better vision than you do. He sees farther than you can, and knows what tomorrow holds as readily as yesterday.

We are focusing on the doubt of Jacob, because even those we perceive as giants of the faith had their moments of doubt. Peter was walking on water when doubt struck him and he began to sink like a stone. Nothing else changed from the moment Peter took his first step upon the waters, to when he began to sink, than that he allowed doubt to make its way into his heart. 'I can't be walking on water, because walking on water is impossible. I'm a fisherman, I've been at sea my whole life, I know what is and isn't within the realm of possibility.'

And so, Peter begins to sink.

Matthew 19:26, "But Jesus looked at them and said to them, 'With men this is impossible, but with God all things are possible.'"

Faith takes us beyond the realm of reason, outside the realm of possibility in the physical, and translates us into God territory, where the impossible happens every day. With men, many things are impossible, with God, all things are possible. Not just most things, not just a handful of things, but all things are possible with God. It took a Man wrestling with Jacob until the break of day and touching the socket of his hip causing it to pop out of joint for Jacob to do away with his doubt once and for all.

Genesis 33:24-25, "Then Jacob was left alone; and a Man wrestled with him until the breaking of day. Now when He saw that He did not prevail against him, he touched the socket of his hip; and the socket of Jacob's hip was out of joint as He wrestled with him."

When we have an intimate encounter with God, everything changes. When we meet God, when we encounter Him in all His glory, we will have convictions not doubts, certainties and not suppositions, faith and not the illusion of faith. We believe in God because we have met Him. We know Him, we know His strength, we know His might, we know His authority, and we know His sovereignty.

God did answer Jacob's prayer, but He answered it in such a way wherein all the planning Jacob had done had been nullified and rendered useless. It turned out Jacob didn't need to split his people into two camps, he didn't need to send his brother various livestock as a gift, and he didn't need to fear, or be distressed. The way God answers our prayers often times highlights the futility of our own endeavors, of our trying to work things out on our own, using our own wisdom and intellect.

Genesis 33:4, "But Esau ran to meet him, and embraced him, and fell on his neck and kissed him, and they wept."

So here was a man who was dreadfully afraid of what his brother would do upon seeing him for the first time in twenty years. I am certain scenarios played through Jacob's mind, one worse than the other, and in his own strength he tried everything he could to shelter himself and his family from the wrath of Esau.

Then Jacob prayed, and God worked it out in such a way, wherein all the preparation Jacob made, was rendered unnecessary and mildly absurd, for his brother Esau ran to meet him, and embraced him, and fell on his neck and kissed him. There was no sword in Esau's hand, there was no bow or spear, there was no violence in him, just love for his brother; a love God had placed there doing away with twenty years' worth of animosity in an instant.

You can try to protect yourself from the violence of men, or pray for God to take the violence from their heart altogether. We fail on our own, or walk victoriously with God, depending on whether or not we truly know Him, trust Him, and humble ourselves before Him.

Exodus 32:11, "Then Moses pleaded with the Lord his God, and said: 'Lord, why does Your wrath burn hot against Your people whom You have brought out of the land of Egypt with great power and with a mighty hand?

CHAPTER THREE
THE PRAYER OF MOSES

F ew if any believers today–or at any time in the past for that matter–would disagree with the notion that by all counts Moses was and is a monolithic figure within the pages of the Old Testament. Even little children, who have only attended a handful of Sunday school classes, can tell you that Moses was the man who parted the Red Sea, and led the people of Israel out of captivity.

Much like little children we have a tendency to focus on the supernatural things God did through Moses, and ignore or marginalize his life up to the point of standing before Pharaoh and demonstrating the power of the Almighty. The life and biography of Moses make for very dramatic reading.

Moses was born in slavery, saved miraculously from death, taught in the school of Pharaoh, but also in the school of God during the forty years he spent in the wilderness. He spends forty years as a prince in Egypt, and another forty as a sheepherder, roaming about the wilderness tending sheep. It is in the desert that God reveals Himself to Moses, and it is also in the desert that Moses begins to understand God has a greater plan for his life than what he had previously envisioned. No life is linear. Each life is extraordinary in its own way, but Moses' life had more twists and turns than most.

As is the case with every servant God chooses for a specific task, Moses had to undergo the process of being stripped of pride and any semblance of arrogance. It is one thing to be born a sheepherder, live as a sheepherder, and die as a sheepherder, it's quite another to go from being a prince to a sheepherder. By all accounts Moses was a man of faith. The Word of God tells us that by faith Moses refused to be called the son of Pharaoh's daughter and chose instead to suffer affliction. In fact, every major decision Moses made in regards to his life was made by faith, and not by sight.

If Moses would have chosen sight over faith or even reason over faith, then he never would have refused to be called the son of Pharaoh's daughter, knowing his only reward for this choice was likely affliction. If Moses were not a man who walked by faith, he never would have forsaken Egypt, because choosing the more difficult path goes against human instinct.

Hebrews 11:24-26, "By faith Moses, when he became of age, refused to be called the son of Pharaoh's daughter, choosing rather to suffer affliction with the people of God than to enjoy the passing pleasures of sin, esteeming the reproach of Christ greater riches than the treasures in Egypt; for he looked to the reward."

By faith we see the true worth of a relationship with God. By faith we realize that the reproach of Christ is a greater fortune than the treasures of Egypt. By faith we look to the reward…a reward that is not forthcoming in this life, but in the life to come.

If the reward of which the author of Hebrews speaks had anything to do with this present life, then Moses would have already received his reward, as you couldn't get much higher up the food chain than being a prince of Egypt at the time. If the reward of which the Word of God speaks had anything to do with the physical or the material, then we could point to Moses and rightly call him foolish for having renounced his princely status, and the treasures of Egypt.

The life of Moses was a life dependent on God…a life tethered to God. Moses was a man who lived under the authority of God daily. It was not something he did on occasion, it was not something he did infrequently, but throughout his life, throughout his journey, we see Moses humbly following God's leadership, and resting under the covering of His authority. Unlike many today, Moses was a man who did not resist God. Today too many individuals, even those who have been called to serve, like to play the I-think-I-can-out-will-God game. Wherever God leads, they have a tendency to resist, or try and steer in a direction of their choosing.

I see this often with mothers and children in stores, especially in the candy isle. If at first their request for chocolate is summarily denied, the children holding their mothers' hands start to pull ever so slightly toward the candy, or the cookies, or the chocolate. All the while they pretend as though nothing untoward is happening, even though the mother can sense she is being tugged in a specific direction. After a while, some mothers will look down at their child and whisper 'stop that,' while others, perhaps not paying enough attention, allow themselves to be dragged to the place the child desired to go to all along.

The only problem is that God is not an inattentive mother who can be manipulated to do what we desire Him to do. God is not distracted or otherwise occupied to the extent He will not notice when we attempt to steer Him toward a different destination than the one He chose for us. Sometimes He whispers 'stop that,' at other times, He leaves us to the desire of our heart just so we'll learn how horribly awry things can go if we do not obey Him, and follow the path He has highlighted for us.

Moses knew there was no better place to be than under the authority of Almighty God. Because of this knowledge, and the faith he possessed, Moses looked upon the treasures and trappings of Egypt and saw them for what they were, realizing that the reproach of Christ is a greater treasure still. Do we behold the things of this earth and see them as Moses did? Do we look upon the material world and prefer the reproach of Christ knowing it is a far greater treasure?

As true believers, as followers of Christ, we must do as Moses did, and choose to suffer affliction with the people of God over enjoying the passing pleasures of sin. Moses did not live an autonomous life. He did not attempt to brave the trials and hardships of his existence on his own, but consistently deferred to God, and asked Him for help and guidance.

It goes without saying that a man who has learned to be dependent upon God, tethered to God, and obedient to God must also have had a vibrant prayer life. If the prayer of Abraham taught us to pray and intercede on behalf of the lost, the prayer of Moses, which we will be discussing al length, teaches us to pray for the household of faith and those who have strayed from the truth.

Both Abraham and Moses interceded on behalf of others, both men had tender hearts for their contemporaries, and both were considered mighty men of God. Perhaps there is a connection between having a tender heart toward those around you, and being a remarkable servant of God. Certain truths become self-evident once we are able to establish a pattern. One such pattern is that all true men and women of God were men and women of prayer. Another such pattern is that they obeyed God even when it wasn't in their flesh's best interest to do so.

So here we have Moses, a man who was tried, tested and proven, having led the people of Israel out of bondage, out of Egypt, and we find them traveling through the desert toward the promised land. Up to this point God had shown His strength and might to the people. It was not as though they were ignorant of what God could do, it was not as though they had not seen Him parting the sea or protecting them. And yet, as Moses went up Mount Sinai to receive the tablets of the Testimony, the people became impatient, and went to Aaron demanding he build them gods to go before them.

Every time I read this particular passage in the Word of God, I am struck by how quickly men forget the goodness of the Lord, and how soon they forget all His benefits. It had not been so long since all the people had seen the army of Pharaoh decimated by the waters of the sea, it had not been so long since they themselves had crossed through the sea as if on dry land, but all of that was in the past, and they were looking toward the future, and Moses was nowhere to be found.

Moses was in fellowship with God. When you are in fellowship with God, you lose track of time. You come before Him, you get on your face and start pouring out your heart, and the next thing you know hours have gone by, and you're in the same spot, still speaking to God and hearing Him speaking to your heart. Such is the relationship Moses had with God. Moses did not come before God out of habit, or duty, or because it was his job, he came before God because he loved Him, and enjoyed spending time in His presence.

We do not serve God out of obligation. We do not spend time in prayer because if we do God will show us favor, or bless us. We spend time in prayer because it is our way of communing and fellowshipping with Him and it is something we look forward to doing each time we get a chance. It didn't take the people long to abandon the God who had been with them, who had saved them, who was for them a pillar of fire by night, and a pillar of cloud by day.

Thinking that their possessions meant more to them than the idol they wanted him to build, Aaron asked the people to break off their golden earrings, and bring them to him. To what I am certain was his surprise, the people brought all their gold before Aaron, and with the gold he made a molded calf. Sad and tragic as the following might sound, it is nevertheless true: men give up their gold for the promise of a false idol, far quicker and with more enthusiasm than they would to the one true God.

In serving their idols, it is assumed that men will have to pay a price. This is why no one complains when they're charged to go see a sporting event, or a concert. When these same individuals are asked to be selfless, and do as Christ commanded, they bristle and begin accusing whoever happens to be standing behind the pulpit of money grubbing, and greed. Thankfully I've never had to take an offering in my life. I have never, not once, stood before a group of people and uttered the words, 'now we're going to take an offering.' Yes, when I travel and preach the pastor usually take up an offering for the ministry at the end of the service, but even then it is a muted and hurried affair. Is it that I'm a secret millionaire? No, not even a secret thousandaire I'm afraid, but there has been so much negative implication concerning preachers and finances, that I would rather not have to deal with it at all.

Somehow, God still provides, and every month the bills get paid, the children in our orphanage get fed, and we are able to continue doing the work to which we have been called. So what's the point of this little detour? Am I trying to defend the money grubbers, and the private-jet-having preachers? No, I'm not, but if you're spending ten times more on your idols than you are sowing into the kingdom of God, perhaps you're not the best person to be appointed judge over others.

Yes, I believe it is more blessed to give than to receive, and I live by this principle. But where you give, is as important as the giving itself. Do not give to have your name etched on a plaque, or to be honored by some prominent minister. Give because God stirs your heart to give, and give wherever He stirs you to give.

Exodus 32:7-10, "And the Lord said to Moses, 'Go, get down! For your people whom you brought out of the land of Egypt have corrupted themselves. They have turned aside quickly out of the way which I commanded them. They have made themselves a molded calf, and worshiped it and sacrificed to it, and said, 'This is your god, O Israel, that brought you out of the land of Egypt!' And the Lord said to Moses, 'I have seen this people, and indeed it is a stiff-necked people! Now therefore, let Me alone, that My wrath may burn hot against them and I may consume them. And I will make of you a great nation.'"

Moses was doing what only a handful of individuals have had the privilege and honor to do in this life, and that is talk to God audibly and directly. The awe Moses must have felt is indescribable, and as he is standing there, basking in the glory of God, God speaks to him and says, 'go, get down!' It wasn't that God no longer wanted to speak to Moses or fellowship with him, but there were pressing matters at the base of the mountain. God knew what the people had done, He knew they had broken faith, and molded a calf which they worshipped and to which they sacrificed.

These were the people of God. People who should have known better, people who should have known they were spurring the wrath of God, but no matter the consequences of their actions, they still proceeded to do what their flesh dictated, which was worship an idol. Although the aforementioned Scripture establishes the context, and tells us why it was that Moses had to intercede on behalf of the people, there are also some practical lessons we would do well to learn from the exchange that took place on Mount Sinai.

The first thing I want to point out, because it goes against the god modern culture has so meticulously fashioned, is that the one true God gets angry. His wrath burns hot against the sons of disobedience, and against those who trample on the blood of His Son. Love is not God's singular attribute. Yes, God is love, but He isn't just love. It is because we've homogenized the idea of God, and who He is, and what He does, that many refuse to believe His own words and warnings, which are clearly spelled out in the Scriptures.

You can read from the Bible, verbatim, without exegesis, without applying systematic theology to the verses you read, and men will still shake their heads and say, 'nope, that can't be God. That's not the god I serve. My god is love, my god wouldn't do that.' This is why false or skewed doctrine is so dangerous. This is why false teachings must be plucked from the root from within the household of faith. Once false teachings and false doctrines take root, once they begin to bloom, then men will no longer believe the very Word of the God they purport to follow and obey.

God gets angry! Unrepentant sin angers Him. Rebellion angers Him. Disobedience angers Him. Idolatry angers Him. There are many things that anger God, not just one, or two, or a handful. In essence God told Moses He needed a minute to destroy the whole of what He called His people, for the rebellion and idolatry they had just exhibited.

Because we no longer believe God gets angry, because we no longer believe He judges, and punishes, and allows His wrath to burn hot, we do not attribute anything of what is going on in America, as well as the world, to Him. 'Well, that couldn't be God... God doesn't do that...God is love, and He wants you to have your best life, and be the best you, you can be.'

No wonder what passes for the church today is so messed up, disjointed, fractured, divided, and worldly. We no longer teach on who God is anymore, even in what ought to be His house, among His people. We have manufactured a palatable God who polls well, and is approved by a great majority, because the God we've manufactured is cuddly, and fuzzy, winks at sin, and gives us stuff.

We are treating God today as the people of Israel did when Moses went up on Mount Sinai. We are indifferent toward Him, think Him impotent, and don't for one second consider that by being idolaters in word and in deed we are daring God to rain judgment upon us. In our stiff-necked, indifferent, and lawless demeanor, we give God no choice but to allow His wrath to burn hot and consume the rebellious and the disobedient. We take God so lightly, and demean the things of God so blatantly that one wonders why it is judgment hasn't already descended, and why in His wrath God has not as yet consumed.

God's wrath was not burning hot against the world, or against those who never knew Him, but against His own, those that ought to have known Him best. The people of God had corrupted themselves, just as many of those calling themselves the people of God today have corrupted themselves. They turned aside from that which God had commanded, just as many calling themselves believers today have turned aside from what God has commanded. Why would we, even for one second, entertain the thought that God will somehow react differently toward our corruption and rebellion than He did toward the people of Israel at the base of Mount Sinai? What makes us think that today God would wink at the sin He was ready to destroy an entire nation for in Moses' day?

God is not mocked...a true and worthwhile lesson for any believer.

God sees the corruption of His people, He sees their divided hearts, He sees the sinfulness toward which they gravitate, and He wholly and unequivocally rejects the justifications they try to use for their rebellion. In their own mind, Israel had a perfectly valid excuse for asking Aaron to make them a god. Moses had gone up on the mountain, and he had not returned. Days had passed—far more days than reasonable—and the people concluded that something must have happened to Moses. Rather than turn their face to the one true God, they demanded other gods of Aaron, gods made by the hands of men, idols which required no obedience, subservience or righteousness.

It's not as though Moses kept the will of God a secret from the people, or was reticent about telling them what God's expectations were. Throughout their journey Moses instructed, and taught, and shared the plan of God, but once we start heading down the path of thinking we know better than God, it is a slippery slope. Not only had the people corrupted themselves, they had turned from the way which God commanded them. In order to be said that someone turned from the way which they were commanded to follow, it is logical to assume they knew the way they ought to have gone.

Having the Word of God takes the notion that we can somehow claim ignorance of God's will off the table completely. We will not be able to stand before Him, shrug our shoulders, and say 'we didn't know that,' because His Word is unambiguous and straightforward. Just as Israel could not excuse their behavior, many who dismiss the word of God and the will of God today, will not be able to excuse their behavior either.

Human nature is surprisingly consistent. Men act and react today just as they did four thousand years ago, because the basic construct of mankind has been such since the beginning of time. No, I don't believe we're evolving. If mankind were evolving, logic would dictate that mankind would be seeking more of God and the knowledge of Him, instead of doing more of what He detests and abhors. Not only have we been shown the way, we have been shown the Christ, the Son of God who came to earth, lived, died, and rose again in order to make a way. No man can claim ignorance of the way, because the way is Jesus, the cornerstone and foundation of our faith.

God speaks, and man refuses to hear. God speaks and man hardens his heart. God shows us the way, and we pretend as though He wasn't clear enough, or the way was not highlighted properly. Once again, God is not mocked. He hasn't grown frail with the passing of time, He hasn't started to miss a step, or be a bit slower than He used to be. He sees all, knows all, perceives all, and when those who are to be His, those who are called by His name become corrupt, stray off the path, and harden their hearts, He grows exceedingly wrathful.

Zechariah 7:11-12, "But they refused to heed, shrugged their shoulders, and stopped their ears so that they could not hear. Yes, they made their hearts like flint, refusing to hear the law and the words which the Lord of hosts sent by His Spirit through the former prophets. Thus great wrath came from the Lord of hosts."

Throughout the history of Israel, this has been a visible and ongoing pattern. God blessed the people, the people began to stray, God began to warn the people, the people refused to heed, God continued warning, the people hardened their hearts, and then finally, the wrath of God was poured out. In His love God pleads with us to repent and return to the path which we have forsaken.

In His love God sends messengers to warn us that if repentance is not forthcoming, judgment certainly will be. Instead of heeding the warnings of God however, we stone the messengers (and then have a love feast to reaffirm that our god is love and love would never do such a thing), and go on doing that which stirred the wrath of God in the first place.

God doesn't send messengers to pat us on the head and tell us how great we are doing. He doesn't send words such as, 'my people, I'm so proud of you for trying; you're doing so well, bravo.' Obedience is expected, it is a given, it is not something with which we impress God; it is the least He expects of those who are called by His name. Righteousness, holiness, humility, selflessness, all these things are expected of us, and if we practice them we are not excelling in the ways of God, we are meeting the minimum requirements.

2 Chronicles 24:19, "Yet He sent prophets to them, to bring them back to the Lord; and they testified against them, but they would not listen."

There have always been, and there will always be consequences to disobedience. There have always been, and there will always be consequences to straying from truth, wandering off the path, and disregarding the words which God speaks in love. God's desire is to bring us back to Himself. Throughout history He has sent prophets to bring the people back to the Lord, and for just as long the people have been stiff-necked and rejected the warnings of God.

Obedience is a choice we make. It is not something we can be forced into doing; it is not something God can twist our arm to do. We choose to obey, we choose to heed His warnings, we choose to humble ourselves, and we choose to repent. What God does is warn whenever we are not walking in the way we ought; but, as far as forcing us to do it? He will not.

When the Scriptures speak of great wrath coming from the Lord of hosts, we tend to forget that this wrath was not aimed at the godless, or those who had no knowledge of Him, but to those who considered themselves the people of God.

When we play games with God, we will always lose. When we discount the Word of God, the warnings of God, and the messages of

God, we will always suffer the consequences of our indifference and apathy.

God had already weighed the people and found them wanting. God had already passed sentence on the whole of Israel, decreeing that His wrath would consume them. And yet Moses begins to intercede for Israel. Moses knew God was right. Moses knew God wasn't making up the details about the people having become corrupt, or abandoning the way which He had commanded them to follow, and yet he still intercedes on their behalf.

Exodus 32:11-13, "Then Moses pleaded with the Lord his God, and said: 'Lord, why does Your wrath burn hot against Your people whom You have brought out of the land of Egypt with great power and with a mighty hand? Why should the Egyptians speak, and say, 'He brought them out to harm them, to kill them in the mountains, and to consume them from the face of the earth?' Turn from Your fierce wrath, and relent from this harm to Your people. Remember Abraham, Isaac, and Israel Your servants, to whom You swore by Your own self and said to them, 'I will multiply your descendants as the stars of heaven; and all this land that I have spoken of I give to your descendants, and they shall inherit it forever.'"

Notice that upon hearing the people had abandoned God, Moses didn't run down the mountain to the people to try and reason with them. He remained in the presence of the Lord, and began to intercede on their behalf. The first thing Moses does is come before the Lord in prayer and supplication on behalf of a people that had given their hearts over to idolatry. Moses pleaded with the Lord his God. We see the personal nature of the relationship Moses had with God. We see that unlike Jacob, who called God, the God of his fathers, Moses knew God intimately and personally.

In order to be able to intercede on behalf of others, God must first be your Lord. When God is Lord of your life, it essentially means He has power, authority and control over you. You are no longer your own, you no longer do as you please; you are a servant beholden to your Lord, doing all He commands you to do. Even though Moses pleaded and interceded on behalf of the people, even though he wanted to see them spared, he also wanted to see honor brought to the name of God. 'Why should the Egyptians speak, and say, 'He brought them out to harm them, to kill them in the mountains, and to consume them from the face of the earth?'

Even when interceding on behalf of others, even when standing in the gap for an entire nation, we must also seek the glory and honor of God. Will our prayer honor God? Will our prayer bring glory to Him? Moses was equally concerned about the people themselves, as he was about what the Egyptians would say concerning the Lord his God. If only the men and women of our day who call themselves sons and daughters of God would be as aware and concerned about the honor and glory of God as Moses was.

Tragically we live in a day and age wherein even those who call themselves shepherds of God's flock have no qualms about heaping shame upon the household of faith, and by relation upon the name of God Himself. It is because such individuals are unconcerned with the glory and honor of the God they purport to serve that they pursue practices and lifestyles unbecoming a child of God.

Even in such a delicate circumstance wherein the fate of an entire nation hung in the balance, the honor and glory of God were still at the forefront of Moses' mind. What a world it would be if all the children of God filtered every decision they made, every word they said, everywhere they went, and everything they did through whether or not it brought honor and glory to God.

It takes boldness to plead with God the way Moses did, especially when he knew the people were deserving of what God had purposed to do. Not once throughout his prayer, did Moses even intimate that God was overreacting, or that somehow the people did not deserve His judgment being poured out upon them. Not once did Moses say 'I think you're being a bit harsh Lord,' because he knew the justice of God, and that in His justice God was justified in consuming the whole of His people.

What we fail to understand, at least from reading this passage in Exodus, is just how much Moses pleaded with God. Near the end of his life, Moses looks back on the journey of God's people, of how God saved them from the hands of the Egyptians, and in the telling of this, he also revisits the time when God had purposed to destroy the nation for its rebellion and sin.

Deuteronomy 8:18-19, "And I fell down before the Lord, as at the first, forty days and forty nights; I neither ate bread nor drank water, because of all your sin which you committed in doing wickedly in the sight of the Lord to provoke Him to anger. For I was afraid of the anger and hot displeasure with which the Lord was angry with you, to destroy you. But the Lord listened to me at that time also."

Forty days and forty nights is how long Moses spent interceding on behalf of Israel so God would not destroy it...forty days and forty nights of no food and no water, just pleading and intercession. When Moses interceded on behalf of Israel, it was by no means a quick and passionless exercise. He didn't just throw up a prayer, hoped God heard it, and made his way down the mountain to get a good view of what was about to happen. Moses pleaded with God. For forty days and forty nights, Moses did nothing else except pray and intercede and hope to change the mind of God regarding consuming the people with His wrath. Because Moses was passionately selfless, he was an effective intercessor. Because Moses cared more for the wellbeing of God's people than his own, God's heart was stirred, and He gave ear to his pleas.

Exodus 32:30-32, "And it came to pass on the next day that Moses said to the people, 'You have sinned a great sin. So now I will go up to the Lord; perhaps I can make atonement for your sin.' Then Moses returned to the Lord and said, 'Oh, these people have sinned a great sin, and have made for themselves a god of gold! Yet now, if You will forgive their sin—but if not, I pray, blot me out of Your book which you have written.'"

Moses was ready to sacrifice himself on behalf of the people. He went before God and asked that his name be blotted from His book if God would not forgive the people their transgression. If ever we needed a definition of what it means to stand in the gap, this is it. God being just, He did not blot Moses' name from His book, but there were consequences to the sins of the people, and those who did sin against the Lord, did have to pay a price.

Exodus 32:33, "And the Lord said to Moses, 'Whoever has sinned against Me, I will blot him out of My book.'"

From this verse we can glean that not all the people of Israel participated in the worship of the golden calf. Not all of them were caught up in the mob mentality, bowing before a graven image and forsaking the God who had guided and led them. Some remained faithful, stood strong, and continued serving God even when the majority went on to worship an idol.

There is a lesson in this for every one of us. God does not judge collectively, He judges individually. The 'everyone else is doing it so I guess it's okay' mentality doesn't cut it with God. His message to Moses was clear: 'whoever has sinned against Me, I will blot him out of My book.' Each of us is accountable for our choices. God will not judge me for the choices you've made, nor will He judge you for the choices I've made. Each of us will stand before God on that great day as individuals, and as individuals we must work out our own salvation with fear and trembling.

Should we pray for each other, intercede on behalf of each other, be a present help for each other, and feel for each other? Most definitively, without equivocation, yes! We can even counsel each other, and lovingly rebuke when we see a brother or a sister straying, but in the end, those who sin against God will be held to account.

Even though Moses prayed, even though he interceded, even though he attempted to atone for the sins of the people, the justice of God is still the justice of God, and He made it clear to Moses that although He relented in His wrath and did not destroy all the people, those who sinned against Him would suffer the consequences of their actions.

God takes no pleasure in the death of the wicked, but the death of the wicked is a direct result and consequence of the sin of which they chose not to repent. It is evident, and beyond doubt that Moses loved people. He loved the people of God, but he also had love in his heart for those who had sinned and rebelled against

God's commandments. It was love that compelled Moses to go up to the Lord, and attempt to make atonement for the people's sins.

When we are servants of God, we love as He loves, and this compels us to intercession and to pleading on behalf of the people more than we would otherwise do for ourselves. Nowhere in the Word of God are we told that Moses interceded for himself for forty days and forty nights, but he did just that on behalf of the people when they sinned against God. The tenderness of one's heart toward the lost says a lot about a man, and reveals the level of his relationship with God.

You cannot love God, and hate God's people. You cannot love God, and be indifferent toward those whom He said He would watch over. There must be a consistency in us in regards to our relationship with our fellow man that cannot be faked or otherwise mimicked. Moses even interceded and pleaded with God for those who spoke evil against him and despised him.

It all started when Moses married an Ethiopian woman. Since Miriam, his sister, and Aaron, his brother, disapproved, they began to speak against Moses. As soon as they began to speak against him, Miriam was struck with leprosy. Moses knew why Miriam had been struck with leprosy. He knew that she, along with their brother, had been speaking against him, yet we find Moses coming before God pleading for her healing.

A lesser man would have pointed to Miriam and said, 'behold, this is what becomes of those who speak against the servant of the Lord,' but Moses prayed for her healing. There is much to be said about the character of a man, when he even prays for his enemies and those that speak against him. May we be spoken of as Moses was, as men and women of integrity and character who seek the face of the Lord on behalf of others.

Even though we might intercede on behalf of someone, and pray for someone, even though we might do as Moses did, and petition God on behalf of those who would speak evil of us, in His sovereign wisdom God might still choose to correct the individual and show them the error of their ways in a direct and forthright matter. Miriam was not spared the punishment of God just because Moses prayed for her. For seven days the leprosy manifested itself, and for seven days the entire Israelite camp knew that Miriam was under the judgment of God. Granted, if Moses would not have prayed, Miriam's leprosy might have been a permanent issue, but there is always consequence to our actions, our disobedience and our rebellion.

Another thing we can learn from the prayer of Moses is that it's not wrong, selfish, or sinful to pray for ourselves. Yes, Moses spent much time in prayer. Yes, Moses spent much time in intercession on behalf of God's people, but he also prayed for himself, petitioning God to show him His way.

> *Exodus 33:13, "Now therefore, I pray, if I have found grace in your sight, show me now Your way, that I may know You and that I may find grace in Your sight. And consider that this nation is Your people."*

Moses didn't pray for possessions, he did not pray for accolades, or glory, fame or position. Moses prayed for God to show him His way, that he might know God all the more, and find even greater grace in His sight. Moses understood what many today simply fail to understand: our relationship with God is ever growing, maturing and expanding. Even though God had told Moses he had found grace in His sight already, and Moses reiterated this fact in his prayer, his one desire was for God's way to be made known to him that he might find even more grace.

Moses desired to grow the intimacy, he desired to grow the relationship between himself and God, and he knew that the only way to do this was to know the way of the Lord and walk therein. Even though we might be called to pray for others, and intercede on behalf of others, we cannot neglect ourselves, or our own spiritual wellbeing.

Yes, there is a danger in being consumed with praying for others to the point that we neglect our own walk, our own spiritual growth, our own relationship, and our own maturing in God. Moses was wise enough to understand that he could only serve God's people if he himself continued to walk in the way of God. If perchance he ceased walking in the way of God, though he might continue to pray for the people and intercede on their behalf, God would no longer answer him because he would no longer be walking in the light.

If my own walk stagnates because I am too concerned with the walk of others, then somewhere along the way I have done something outside of God's will. From a purely human perspective we might not see anything wrong with being consumed with our calling, but if it takes away from our relationship with God, then God sees something wrong with it.

Relationship comes first. It always has, and it always will. It is because the men and women of the Bible had an established relationship with God that He was able to use them in great and mighty ways. They were men and women of prayer who knew God, and who loved God first. It is out of that love and knowledge that obedience was birthed, and because obedience was birthed in them God was able to work glorious works through them.

There is much wisdom in the prayer Moses prayed for himself, as well as a real and visible dependency on God. Moses did not pray for God to show him the easiest way, the fastest way, the least troublesome way, or the most scenic way. Moses prayed for God to show him His way, for only in the way of God, only in obedience and subservience to Him will we walk surefootedly, possessing the knowledge that we are walking toward the right destination.

More often than not, when the way of the Lord gets difficult, or seems to require effort on our part, we tend to try and make our own way, find a circuitous route, and avoid the exertion required to follow the way of God. We think ourselves wise in our own eyes, having of our own volition spared ourselves some sort of difficulty by forging our own path, not realizing that though the way of the Lord seemed difficult, there would also be a blessing and a grace along the way for those who walked it. We get so caught up in following the way of a denomination or a certain preacher, and tragically, often even the way of the world, that we dismiss and disregard the way of the Lord thinking it irrelevant.

In the way of the Lord there is grace. In the way of the Lord there is mercy. In the way of the Lord there is peace, there is joy, and there is strength. No matter how good our own paths might seem to our own eyes, no matter how good the way of a denomination or a certain church might seem, if it is not in harmony with the way of the Lord, it will lead to ruination and despair.

May the cry of our heart be as that of Moses, 'show me now Your way, that I may know You.'

Isaiah 55:9, "For as the heavens are higher than the earth, so are My ways higher than your ways, and my thoughts higher than your thoughts."

The ways of the Lord will always differ from the ways of man. The ways of the Lord will always be higher than our ways and as such our prayer must be that the Lord show us His ways, rather than accept or validate our own. The way of the Lord is certain. There is no second guessing or confusion when we allow Him to lead us, and we follow after Him as obedient children. It is when man takes it upon himself to seek after a different way, or forge for himself a different path that confusion becomes a constant companion and second guessing a way of life.

Before the invention of the global positioning system, men and women alike actually had to rely on maps or road signs for their directions. Not that the global positioning system is a cure-all, because once in a while you hear stories of how some unfortunate soul or another ended up driving into a lake or a river because they were following their GPS. By and large however, the machine is accurate, and it will get you to your destination.

The difference between a GPS and God is that God is always accurate. Sometimes, His way will lead us through places and situations where the flesh will begin to scream and reason will begin to moan to us that if we continue to follow the course we happen to be on, it will lead to nothing but heartache and sorrow. It is then that we must disregard our own senses, our own reason, and trust fully in God our Father. We either trust God, or our flesh. We either follow the predetermined way God has set before us, or we lean on our own understanding and veer of the path that has been marked and highlighted for us.

If the prayer of our heart is for God to show us His way, it's not so we might analyze and compare it to our own path, it is not to have a second option once our first choice fails miserably, it is to follow it, and in following it we will know Him all the more. The way of God is a holy way, it is a righteous way, and only the righteous can walk upon it, while the rebellious and duplicitous veer off and seek another way.

The way of God is singular. The way is Christ, and no man comes to the Father but by Him. The instant we allow ourselves to be open to the possibility that there is another way to God but through Christ, we make Jesus a liar and His sacrifice of no effect. Hence the reason we must desire wholeheartedly that His will be done in our lives, that His way be shown to us so we might walk upon it, and not attempt to impose our will upon God. Moses prayed for God to show him His way that he might know Him, and find grace in His sight.

When we take into account that this was the selfsame man who heard God speaking to him in a burning bush, who by God's command led His people out of Egypt, who had spent forty days in the presence of God, who spoke to God, and had a more intimate knowledge of Him than most men dare to imagine, it is humbling to see his desire remain the knowledge of God.

No man or woman living today can claim to know God on the level Moses did, yet few if any of us pray to know God more on a consistent basis. We have other things we deem more important or time sensitive to pray about, and the knowledge of God, and the desire thereof, always seems to get pushed to the back of the line, and the bottom of the list. No matter how far along we think ourselves to be, no matter how much we know of God, there is always more of Him to be discovered. We grow in the knowledge of God by continually being in His presence, and desiring to know Him better. When our desire is to know God, we are not distracted by other issues. We do not desire other things since our sole focus is the knowledge of Him. Once this occurs in the heart, we realize just how futile desiring anything else but Him truly is, and how much time we've wasted throughout the years chasing after something other than God.

Exodus 33:18, 'And he said, 'Please, show me Your glory.'

The knowledge of God stirs within us the desire to see the glory of God. There is no such thing as contentedness when it comes to our relationship with God. We never come to a point in our walk, in our knowledge of Him, or our relationship with Him, wherein we are satisfied, and desire no more. With each new revelation God pours into our hearts, with each new glimpse of Him, with each new whisper, our desire for Him and the knowledge of Him and the glory of Him only grows and intensifies.

If our desire to know more of God has waned, if we have substituted something else for wanting to see His glory, then it is incumbent upon us to search our hearts in the light of the gospel and see where we have strayed, and where we have allowed the enemy to sidetrack us, and detour our spiritual journey. To desire to know God and His glory is the natural state of a child of God. We are neither abnormal nor aberrant in our desire for more of God in our lives. It is not wanting or desiring to know Him more, it is not wanting or desiring to see His glory that is uncharacteristic and anomalous, yet somehow we've twisted this aspect of our faith as we have so many others throughout the years.

Every one of Moses's requests was of a spiritual nature. First he desired to be shown the way of God, then he desired to know God Himself, and finally he asked God to show him His glory. Throughout his prayer, Moses never requested anything tethered to this present world, because he had realized the futility of the material long ago when he abandoned being a prince in the house of Pharaoh for being a sheepherder in the desert.

Exodus 33:19, "Then He said, 'I will make all My goodness pass before you, and I will proclaim the name of the Lord before you. I will be gracious to whom I will be gracious, and I will have compassion on whom I will have compassion.'"

It is only when we realize what the glory of God is, that we can conclude it has been shown to us as it was shown to Moses. God Himself defines His glory as His graciousness and compassion. We see His graciousness, we see His compassion, we see His goodness pass before us as Moses did if only we choose to open our eyes and see them for what they are. In order to be able to see the glory of God, we must be near Him. We cannot live with the expectation of seeing or experiencing the glory of God, while being far from His will, far from His purpose and walking away from Him rather than toward Him.

As simplistic and rudimentary as the preceding might sound, there are many believers today who desire to see the glory of God, and all that it entails without being in the will of God, and about their callings. The glory of God and the person of God are inexorably linked and we cannot experience one without the other. This is why any spiritual movement that does not have Jesus as its focus, cornerstone, nexus and linchpin, cannot succeed, thrive, or perpetuate, because they are attempting the impossible...namely possessing the glory without submitting to God.

Exodus 33:21, 'And the Lord said, 'Here is a place by Me, and you shall stand on the rock.'"

Whenever we stand near God and behold His glory, it transforms us. One cannot behold the glory of God and remain the same. Even those around us will see the difference, and wonder if only to themselves what the catalyst for this change might have been. Moses spent forty days and forty nights in the presence of God. For these forty days and forty nights God sustained him since he neither drank water nor ate bread. Yet, when Moses came down the mountain the skin on his face shone, and the children of Israel were afraid to come near him.

Exodus 34:28-30, "So he was there with the Lord forty days and forty nights; he neither ate bread nor drank water. And He wrote on the tablets the words of the covenant, the Ten Commandments. Now it was so, when Moses came down from Mount Sinai (and the two tablets of the Testimony were in Moses' hand when he came down from the mountain), that Moses did not know that the skin of his face shone while he talked with Him. So when Aaron and all the children of Israel saw Moses, behold, the skin on his face shone, and they were afraid to come near him."

Being in the presence of the Lord, spending time with Him, and seeing His glory are undeniably visible on the countenance of the individual. One cannot be in the presence of God and not show signs of this reality. We are transformed in His image, and grow from glory to glory when we stand in the presence of the Lord. Both inwardly and outwardly, the glory of God is visible and palpable. The people saw the countenance of Moses, they saw his skin shining, and they were afraid to come near him because they did not understand what this meant.

By the same token, Moses was unaware that the skin on his face shone while he talked with God. The presence of God, and the visible glory of God in us and upon us, need not be something we ourselves highlight, or attempt to draw attention to. Moses didn't go around telling people to look a little closer to see how his face shone; the man didn't even know this was happening to him.

It's always off-putting when men attempt to lift themselves up, or glorify themselves because of something God did in them or through them. We have adopted the mentality of the world when it comes to the work of God, and rather than being humble that God might raise us up, we claw and scrape and climb our way to the top as viciously, cunningly and mercilessly as those of the world. We fail to understand that any glory we appropriate for ourselves will be nothing more than bitter ash in our mouths, and any kingdom we build for ourselves will be nothing more than ruination.

God is not mocked. He sees all things, He knows all things, yes even the hidden things of the heart, and if we attempt to use the glory of God for our own benefit, then we will suffer the consequences of our deceitfulness in due season. To have the glory of God be so heavy upon you that your skin is shining, and you not even noticing, is a humbling and remarkable thing. Moses was so consumed with being in the presence of God, that he didn't notice how having been in His presence changed him.

When we are in the presence of God everything else fades into obscurity. We realize our own insignificance, our own fragility and impotence, while seeing the grandeur of our God in its true light, and being all the more humbled by it. There is no more life changing an event than being witness to the glory of God, and knowing this, Moses prayed that he might see it.

Moses was an imperfect man who trusted in the perfection of God. He was a man for whom humility was a way of life and whose dependency upon God remained constant throughout his journey. Did Moses make mistakes? Of course he did. He was, after all, a man. But the desire of his heart was always more of God in his life, and God honored this. When we are in the presence of no one but God and begin to intercede on behalf of others, whether a family member, a friend, or an entire nation, our true heart is revealed. Men might feign piety when among other believers, they might feign righteousness when the situation requires it, but there is no profit or benefit in feigning intercession on behalf of others, especially when it's just you in your prayer closet or your secret place.

In both intent and deed, Moses possessed a pure heart, and desired to see the salvation of the people of Israel. There was no other reason for him to intercede the way he did, with the passion he exhibited, going so far as to put himself in danger for the sake of the people, if Moses did not possess true and lasting love for them. Beholding the world as it is, one would find plenty of excuses to turn their back on the whole thing, find a quiet place somewhere in the foothills of a mountain range, and live out the rest of their life in solitude, just them and God and a few basic necessities. Love, however, compels us to stand in the gap, to hold the line, and to pray ceaselessly that God open the eyes of the blind, stir hearts to repentance, and cause those who thus far have refused to hear the gospel of Christ, to open their hearts toward it.

We pray and intercede on behalf of others, because the Word of God confirms time and again, that intercession works. When we intercede on behalf of others, and live with the expectation of having our prayers answered, we do so not because they are good, but because God is good.

Exodus 34:9, "Then he said, 'If now I have found grace in Your sight, O Lord, let my Lord, I pray, go among us, even though we are a stiff-necked people; and pardon our iniquity and our sin, and take us as Your inheritance.'"

Moses did not try to sugar coat the reality of the people's spiritual condition, nor did he try to approach God with the 'they're good people' paradigm. Moses knew that the omniscience and justice of God prevented him from being able to highlight the people's virtues, so Moses appealed to the mercy of God instead. Moses acknowledged the stubbornness of the people, as well as their iniquity and sin, and rather than attempt to justify it, minimize it, overlook it or ignore it, he asked for God's pardon and guidance instead.

One could more readily hide the midday sun than men hide their iniquities and sins from the eyes of God. All knowing is by definition all encompassing, and since God is all knowing our attempt to either justify our iniquity or pretend it does not exist, elicits the anger of God.

One other aspect of the prayer of Moses I have always found intriguing, and one that is a worthwhile lesson for us all, is that Moses was not content to have any surrogates. Moses did not settle for an angel. He prayed, and earnestly so, that the Lord Himself, His presence, be with His people, for only in this way would it be known that they had found grace in His sight.

Exodus 33:15-16, "Then he said to Him, 'If your Presence does not go with us, do not bring us up from here. For how then will it be known that Your people and I have found grace in Your sight, except You go with us? So we shall be separate, Your people and I, from all the people who are upon the face of the earth."

The only way the world will know we are separate from all the people who are upon the face of the earth, is if the Presence of the Lord is with us. It is the Presence of God, the Holy Spirit dwelling in the heart of the individual that identifies him as sanctified and set apart, and that separates him from all others. Moses wanted the world to see this distinction among the people of God. He wanted the world to know that they were indeed a peculiar people, a separate people, a people who served their God and whose God protected them and kept them.

It befuddles me that although the Word of God clearly tells us we are to be a separate and peculiar people, the modern day church is going out of its way to amalgamate and ingratiate itself to the world. May we rejoice in that we are a separate people from all the people who are upon the face of the earth. May we rejoice in the reality that the presence of our God in our midst and in our hearts makes us separate and unique.

What makes us separate and unique is not a fish sticker on our back bumper, it is not a membership pin from a particular denomination...it is the Presence of God. If His Presence does not go before us, then there is no point to any of what we do. If His Presence does not go before us, then all our endeavors are futile, our machinations vain, and our proclamations vapid. Moses knew this as well as any hero of the Bible, and he tailored his prayers in such a way that consistently and continually the presence and will of God for himself as well as the nation of Israel was foremost in his petitions.

Joshua 7:7 "And Joshua said, 'Alas, Lord God, why have You brought this people over the Jordan at all – to deliver us into the hand of the Amorites, to destroy us?

CHAPTER FOUR
THE PRAYER OF JOSHUA

Before being the consummate warrior, leader of men, and one possessing the high honor of having had dialogue with God Himself, Joshua was a servant, an aide and understudy to Moses. For forty years Joshua served faithfully and before Moses dies, God tells Moses to commission Joshua to lead the people into the Promised Land.

Joshua was faithful, and his faithfulness was rewarded in due season. He never attempted to take power for himself, or dispossess Moses of his authority in his latter years; he served in the capacity of his office, until God saw fit to promote him to a higher office still.

Of the many lessons the life of Joshua can teach us, this is perhaps the most profound, yet most often overlooked of all: be content with where God has positioned you. Be content in the calling to which you were called, do the work with which you were entrusted to the best of your ability, with all your heart, and the day will come when having been faithful in the little, God will require greater things still.

We spend so much time trying to plot and plan and inch our way up the ladder. We don't realize it is God who promotes, it is God who calls to a higher office, and if we would have spent the time just being faithful to the calling to which we are presently called, we would have been promoted long ago. The difference between man promoting himself, and God promoting him, is evident: when man promotes himself it is a difficult thing, like slogging through a muddy field, but when God promotes a man, it comes about with ease, and in such a way wherein everyone can see the hand of God at work.

Before one can lead, they must first learn how to serve. Before one can be entrusted with great things, they must first prove themselves faithful in the little things. If you trusted someone with a dollar, and they betrayed your trust, then you know that giving them ten thousand dollars would result in the same sort of betrayal. If however, you entrusted someone with a dollar, and they lived up to your expectation, then you know you can trust them with more.

Little things are tests on our way to greater things. This is why we must not despise what we would deem lesser callings, but faithfully set about doing our duty and being faithful in the calling to which we are called. Some are called to preach, others are called to pray, others to vacuum the sanctuary after everyone has left, but no one calling is less than another, for all of them work together toward the glory of God and furthering of His kingdom. God sees the act of obedience and faithfulness of an individual, not what it was they were obedient in. God rewards obedience in its purest form, regardless of what He commanded of the individual.

Not only did Joshua serve at the behest of Moses, he learned from him, and applied that which he learned throughout his hundred and ten year life. It's not enough to have a good example, it is not enough to have a good role model, if we reject their counsel and set about following a different path than that upon which they walked.

Joshua knew Moses was a man of God, he saw the power of God in the life of Moses, he saw what God did through him, and desired to be used in like manner when his time came. Because Joshua desired to be used of God as Moses was, he applied the same virtues and practices he had seen Moses practicing, one of which was consistent and heartfelt prayer.

The life of Joshua in its entirety is an awe inspiring one, seeing as he was close to 90 years of age when God called him to lead the people. When most individuals would be well into their retirement, God calls Joshua to lead Israel, not during peacetime, but during a season wherein their enemies were plentiful and the battles they had to wage became some of the most talked about military campaigns ever waged.

The life of Joshua also confirms what many have known for generations: that being a warrior and being a man of prayer are not mutually exclusive. One would be hard pressed to find a military mind as brilliant as Joshua's in the Bible, or a more consummate soldier for that matter, but Joshua is also a man who prayed often, obeyed without complaint, and kept faith with the promises of God even when others doubted them.

What endears me most to Joshua took place early on in his life, when he, along with Caleb, and ten others were sent to spy out the land of Canaan. For forty days these men spied on the land of their enemies, and when they returned, all but two namely, Caleb and Joshua, gave reports of frightful giants whom they could not hope to overcome.

Joshua and Caleb remembered the promises of God, and stood on them. They did not see the giants as an obstacle that could not be overcome, but rather as an opportunity for God to show His power once more. Depending on whether or not we stand on the promises of God, we will either see the obstacles in our lives as insurmountable, or as an opportunity to see the glory of God. It was upon reading this passage in the Scriptures many years ago, that I was instantly drawn to Joshua, his life, his leadership, and his relationship with God.

Although there are many prayers Joshua prayed throughout his life, we will be discussing one prayer in particular. It is a prayer he prayed after being beaten back at the gates of Ai, even though Jericho, a far stronger and more imposing city had just been vanquished.

When it comes to prayer, there are three possible outcomes. The first possible outcome is that God answers the prayer immediately, the second that He delays in answering our prayer, and the third, is that He chooses not to answer at all, or rejects it. Yes, God can say no to our prayers, and though it is difficult for us as individuals every time He does so, we must rest in the knowledge that He knows best.

We have examples of each of these outcomes within the pages of Scripture, and as we progress and continue with our series, we will see these outcomes as self-evident. I mention this because I've heard it said by men who many would consider our spiritual betters, that God is mandated to answer every prayer we pray, and if He doesn't do so the first time, well, then we try, try again until we somehow manage to twist His arm into doing our bidding. Not only is this wrong, it is unscriptural, and there are countless souls today praying for things which are not in accordance with God's will, and growing frustrated because God isn't answering them even though the man with the shiny teeth on television told them God must.

Misconception and a skewed understanding of Biblical principles, as well as fundamental doctrines of the faith, create skewed believers whose priorities and ideals are in direct opposition to what the Word of God says our principles and ideals as children of God ought to be. Whether we want to acknowledge it or not, the fact remains that God can say 'no' to us and deny us something we really wanted, because He knows it would do us more harm than good. I realize full well that some individuals have never been denied anything in their lives so the concept of God denying them something is anathema to them, but nevertheless, it happens, and with great regularity.

On a tangentially related side note, it's the children whom the parents never uttered 'no' to in their adolescence who end up some of the most shipwrecked and hopeless souls walking the planet today. You see it in what many like to refer to as former child stars that grow up and realize the world is not their oyster, and that they really can't have everything they ever wanted, to children from well-to-do families, for whom parenting and discipline were abstract notions that did not directly impact them.

Being said no to from time to time, is healthy and necessary. God knows this better than we can ever hope to, and this is why, when the situation warrants it, He tells us no.

Having been a soldier all his life, Joshua knew how to follow orders. As such, he also knew to accept being denied, or being said no to, whether by Moses, his direct superior for much of his life, or by God, his superior's superior. Because of his faithfulness and obedience, Joshua was one of two individuals to have left Egypt, and likewise entered the Promised Land. An entire nation had left Egypt, an entire nation had crossed the Red Sea, yet because they did not believe, because they doubted, and gave their hearts to idols, everyone except for Joshua and Caleb died in the desert on their way to the Promised Land.

A journey that ought to have taken forty days, ended up taking forty years, because only those pure of heart are received into God's promise.

Throughout this protracted journey Joshua learned to follow, but he also learned to lead. Trusting in the arm of the Lord, and being obedient in all things, Joshua racks up some stunning victories, going so far as to take Jericho, a city that had been securely shut up, and considered impregnable. All who had been present knew the conquest of Jericho was the Lord's doing. They had seen the wall fall down flat before them, yet even after seeing God supernaturally bring down the wall of Jericho, and being told with specificity to keep themselves from the accursed things, there was one who transgressed and disobeyed.

What we will come to understand shortly, and this is important because of how God views a nation or a people, is that although one man sinned, God considered that the whole of Israel had sinned against Him.

As usual, however, I get ahead of myself.

Jericho had been vanquished, the city and all that was in it burned with fire except for the silver, gold, and vessels of bronze and iron, which had been put into the treasury of the house of the Lord, and Israel with Joshua at the forefront set its sights on Ai, a far smaller town than the one they had just conquered.

At first, as was his custom, Joshua, ever the warrior, sent spies to Ai to gauge their strengths, their weaknesses, and see how difficult they would be to vanquish. From a military tactic standpoint this was sound practice, but what Joshua could not know, and what his spies could not foresee was the fact that the anger of the Lord had burned against the children of Israel because one among them had committed a trespass regarding the accursed things.

As spies, men trained to observe, record, and report that which they had seen, the men came back and reported to Joshua that the people of Ai were few, and it would not be productive to bring all the people against them. In their estimation, three thousand men would be more than enough to vanquish Ai, and take yet another city.

Wisdom would dictate that we see the spiritual component in this event, and realize that there is more than meets the eye to certain things. What we might deem as irrelevant or readily scalable often times turns into a protracted nightmare, because we did not bother to see the problem through the prism of the spiritual, but only through the prism of the physical.

As per the advice of his men Joshua sent a contingent of three thousand, fully expecting to have them return victorious. As is often the case, we are all the more affected by a certain event in our lives, when we expected the complete opposite to transpire. If I go on a diet for two weeks, and instead of dropping a few pounds the scale shows me that I've gained a couple, because I expected the diametrically opposite result than what I got, I will be all the more disappointed and upset.

I mention this, because some learned men and theologians can't seem to wrap their minds around why it was that Joshua became so distraught, going so far as to tear his clothes and fall to the floor. Joshua had expected an unmitigated victory, and what he got instead was an unmitigated defeat. This is the reason he was so upset, and why his reaction to having lost a battle seemed so out of place, especially for one who was used to battle, and to seeing the dead and the wounded.

The handful of souls at Ai, those of whom his own spies said were unworthy of the entire army requiring only a small contingent to do the job, put down the three thousand seasoned warriors Joshua had sent to flight. Not only did Joshua's soldiers flee from before the men of Ai, the men of Ai proceeded to chase them from before the gate as far as Shebarim.

Although the distance from the gates of Ai to Shebarim is unknown, what is known is that the attacking force retreated, and those who had been on the defensive, went on the offensive and gave chase, striking Israel's army as it fled. It is one thing to send unseasoned men into battle and have their hearts melt and become like water, it's quite another to see seasoned soldiers act in such a manner.

Having seen battle before, the fear Joshua's soldiers felt was not a natural fear, but one that had been put there by God, because His anger burned hot against the people for their transgression. You could have a bigger army, be better equipped, have the tactical advantage, be seasoned in warfare, and still flee from before a smaller, less equipped, and less experienced foe if God is not on your side.

No matter the circumstance, no matter the situation, it is God who gives the victory. It is the same with every nation, throughout every generation, wherein we witness certain key moments, and can only conclude that the hand of God was at work, and a sovereign, supernatural intervention took place.

One can likewise frequently observe that when the nation to which God gave victory begins to beat its metaphorical chest and take the credit for something God did, or disavow itself of God altogether, He removes His hand of blessing and protection, showing them the futility of their machinations when His aid is no longer present.

It is a horribly sinking feeling to realize that having done everything right, as far as human reason is concerned, things could not have possibly turned out any worse in your endeavor. The wise among us recognize the hand of God, search their hearts, and repent, while the proud and foolish among us shake their fists at Him in the ultimate show of futility, blaming Him for what they forced Him to do. As individuals and as a people, we reap what we sow, and if we have sown rebellion, disobedience, hedonism, perversion, and vanity we will reap the burning anger of the Lord against us.

News of Israel's defeat reached Joshua, and recognizing the hand of God in what had just transpired, Joshua went before the Lord. Joshua did not approach the Lord attempting to justify the people's rebellion, nor did he ask God for an explanation as to why the people had been defeated. He came before God in humility and brokenness, knowing the justice of God, and realizing God does nothing without ample cause.

Joshua 7:6, "Then Joshua tore his clothes, and fell to the earth on his face before the ark of the Lord until evening, both he and the elders of Israel; and they put dust on their heads."

Considering that as yet Joshua did not know that the children of Israel had committed a trespass regarding the accursed things, and knowing himself to have been faithful to God both in the small things and the great ones, one can't help but wonder what was going through his mind as he heard of Israel's defeat. It is one thing to know ourselves as having been guilty of something, having done something to transgress or displease God, but to know oneself innocent of evil, innocent of guile or sin, and still see the hand of God pressing down with severity, is something simultaneously humbling and vexing.

All Joshua knew was that his army had been defeated when all the evidence pointed to an easy victory. All he knew was that the hearts of his soldiers had melted and became like water, but as yet he did not know the reason for this. Even so, both Joshua, and the elders of Israel fell to the earth on their faces before the ark of the Lord, and put dust on their heads.

Little is spoken about the sovereignty of God nowadays, because we like to think ourselves masters of our own destiny. Because we have removed the notion of sovereignty from the attributes of God, whenever something unexpected happens, rather than falling on our faces before Him, humbling ourselves, and crying out, we react instinctively, becoming indignant and proceed to go about trying to convince God that He got it wrong. Rather than humbly asking God to show us why He had to do what He did, we attempt to fault God, and justify our actions, concluding that His correction was too harsh and unloving.

Because Joshua knew God, and intimately so, he knew that God hadn't gotten it wrong, that God hadn't overreacted, but that what had just taken place was warranted and deserved. Having seen the defeat of his three thousand man contingent, Joshua now came before the Lord in humility, waiting on Him to speak.

It is not sin to ask God to clarify something we do not understand. It is however sin to tell God He is mistaken, and what He deemed appropriate is by human standard too harsh.

Joshua 7:7-9, "And Joshua said, 'Alas, Lord God, why have You brought this people over the Jordan at all – to deliver us into the hand of the Amorites, to destroy us? Oh, that we had been content, and dwelt on the other side of the Jordan! O Lord, what shall I say when Israel turns its back before its enemies? For the

*Canaanites and the inhabitants of the land will hear of it, and
surround us, and cut off our name from the earth. Then what will
You do for Your great name?'"*

It is human nature to resort to asking why, whenever we do
not understand or fully perceive something. Joshua, as faithful, committed, obedient and consistent as he was, was still human and so
he came before God with the burning question of why. Life on this
earth is not linear. There are valleys, as well as hills, there are moments of rapturous exaltation as well as moments of unimaginable
desperation, there are moments of wondrous victories, as well as moments of unforeseen defeats, and together they make up what we
have come to refer to as human existence.

No, Christians are not spared valleys, they are not spared
hardships, and they are not spared moments of uncertainty or dis-
quiet. We are human; therefore we will have such moments in life.
What God promises, and what separates us from the rest of the
world, is that He will be with us throughout our journey, whether on
the mountaintop or in the valley, and if need be we can lean on Him,
go to Him for comfort, help, peace, and healing. If we live our lives
expecting never to have to endure or go through hardships, it's only
a matter of time before we are crushed and disappointed, unable to
shake the feeling of somehow being let down.

Upon experiencing victory of any kind, most individuals will
act in a predictable and anticipated manner. We'll smile, we'll clap
a little, perhaps breathe a sigh of relief, and generally show genuine
joy.

It is upon experiencing defeat that reactions vary, and do
so wildly. When someone suffers a setback or a defeat– especially
one on the scale of the one Joshua had just suffered–the reaction of
the individual cannot be predicted or anticipated. Some are simply
shell-shocked at first, unable to process what just happened, others
ignite as though someone just lit their fuse, others scream, others cry,
because raw emotion is by its definition unpredictable and erratic.

Defeat, setback, or rejection in any area of life is unpleasant.
Seeing as no one likes to lose or be defeated, it is wisdom itself to see
if we can somehow avoid or drastically reduce being defeated in life.

What led to Israel's defeat? What did they do (or not do) to warrant their being vanquished by a smaller and less prepared foe?

The first thing both Joshua and Israel failed to do was pray before making the decision to go up and attack Ai.

Although Joshua was usually a man of consistent prayer, when it came to Ai he had a lapse in judgment, a moment of inattentiveness, wherein he did not go before God and ask concerning Ai, but proceeded to take the advice of his spies and sent a contingent to defeat it. One of the most important lessons we can learn from this period in Joshua's life is that even when something looks like a guaranteed win, a surefire thing, a slam dunk, or any other overused cliché one might think of, go before God and ask Him anyway. Do not circumvent prayer just because something looks easy, or the way ahead is too obvious to require God's blessing or direction. If God's ways are not our ways, then logic would dictate the path we would choose isn't necessarily the path He would choose.

Perhaps it was just an oversight on Joshua's part, or he saw what he thought was a clear victory and decided not to go before God and ask for His blessing. Either way, the absence of prayer, the absence of asking God what it was he must do after the conquest of Jericho, contributed to Israel's defeat at Ai.

We tend to ask God when it comes to big decisions. We tend to take a few days of fasting, and pray whenever we have to decide on whether or not we're going to change jobs, or move halfway across the country, or to another continent. When it comes to life changing, life altering decisions, we do pray and seek the face of God until He answers, but when it comes to smaller issues, we have the tendency to bypass prayer as Joshua did, often times with the same results.

Another dangerous practice of many believers is living off the victories of the past, and allowing them to propel us onward without taking the time to inquire of God. sWe become so blinded by yesterday's successes, so enamored with ourselves for having overcome yesterday's hurtles, that we attempt to take the credit for these things, and willfully pretend as though it was not the hand of God which carried us through.

Because we talk ourselves into believing we did it all on our own, we did it all by ourselves, and have by default become masters of our destinies and captains of our own ships, we no longer go before God and ask His blessing, because in our estimation the previous victories were all our own doing. We cannot live in the present by drawing strength from our nostalgic past. We cannot walk today, in the victories of yesteryear, because each day is a battle, each day is a confrontation, and each day we either conquer or are vanquished.

It is an easy thing to get caught up in reliving the past, in fondly remembering the courage, boldness, and focus we had in our younger years, but it is unproductive, and often times destructive to relive the past without focusing on the present. I grew up in a time and in a country wherein the power of God moved in ways rarely seen in today's western nations. There were healings, there was prophecy, there were miracles, there were dreams, and visions, and the power and gifts of the Holy Spirit were made manifest often, and in an undeniable manner. It was also a time of persecution wherein the children of God were imprisoned, tortured, beaten, stripped of their earthly possessions and even killed, and their only hope, their only refuge was the presence and power of God.

It would be easy for me to stand behind a pulpit and retell stories of the past. The people would enjoy it far more readily than they do the messages on repentance God often compels me to speak. I would have a lot more friends, and the ministry would be much larger than it is.

The only problem with living in the past is that we tend to forget about the present. I don't want to live the rest of my life telling stories of what I saw in my childhood as far as miracles, prophecies, and healings are concerned. I want to see them today, in this time, and I know it is possible because God has not changed, and neither have His promises. Winning a battle does not winning the war make! Many a soul forgets this simple truth, and after obtaining one victory in an area of their lives, they go on to suffer three or four subsequent defeats, because they started neglecting prayer, fasting, the Scriptures, and their relationship with God after that first initial victory. 'Apart from Me, you can do nothing.' These were the words of Jesus, and they were not intended to be anything more than what they are…the truth. These words held true two thousand years ago, and they hold true today.

No matter how confident we might be in our own abilities, no matter how self-reliant, self-assured, or self-possessed, apart from Christ, we can do nothing. It's when we start meditating upon certain things Jesus said, and understanding their ramifications, that we begin to understand how anti-scriptural and destructive some of the most popular doctrines floating about today truly are.

Jesus said that apart from Him we can do nothing, but men on television are telling us every day that, in and of ourselves, we have every resource we need to live our best lives, and excel at everything we put our hand to. And herein we see the second thing that contributed to Israel's defeat at Ai: overconfidence. They were so enthused and galvanized by the victory at Jericho that in their thinking as well as their actions the people became overconfident. We perceive this overconfidence both in the words the spies spoke in regards to Ai, as well as Joshua's quick decision to send three thousand men to conquer the city without asking God first.

There is nothing wrong with confidence, as long as your confidence is anchored in Christ. There is nothing wrong with confidence as long as you are confident in God's abilities and not your own.

There is an old saying, but in my estimation a true saying, that the man who is confident in himself has confidence in a fool. I realize full well this flies in the face of modern teaching, wherein every individual is the nexus of their own universe, the apple of God's eye, the reason all things were created and are maintained, but Scripture still stands as testament that whenever men were confident in themselves, they failed miserably at whatever task stood before them. One of the most vivid examples of overconfidence, and the ensuing consequences thereof, was Peter the Apostle of Christ, also known as the rock upon which Jesus said He would build His church.

Jesus was not shy about telling His apostles what the future held. He was not shy about telling them that He would have to suffer, and die, and in the process be abandoned by all. Although the others kept silent, and meditated on what Jesus had said, Peter speaks up and says, 'even if I have to die with you, I will not deny you!'

Bold words, confident words, empty words. We know, from reading the Word of God, that Peter denied Christ not once, not twice, but three times, and not before of some magistrate or authority, but before a servant girl who had suggested that he knew Jesus. If I trust in my own power, if I trust in my own strength, if I trust in my own wisdom, abilities or prowess, my failure is assured even before I begin my endeavor. To God all things are possible, but to man even the possible becomes impossible when he trusts in himself.

1 Corinthians 10:12, "Therefore let him who thinks he stands take heed lest he fall."

It may seem like I'm harping on this specific point, but if it is so, then it is with a purpose. I have seen many an individual conquer their Jericho, only to be vanquished by Ai, because they did not inquire of God, trust in God, or depend on God. I have known individuals who stood in the face of persecution, loss, and exile, only to succumb to greed or the glory of men.

In tracing back the reason for their fall, one concludes that although they prayed and sought the face of God in their hardship, they neglected to do so in their time of comfort and excess. Seek God always, and you will stand in Him and the power of His might. If we are honest with ourselves, and think back just on the last week, we will be amazed at how many decisions we've made without consulting God, or asking God whether or not we should proceed with a given idea or plan. One decision without consulting God leads to two, two lead to four, and only when we've thoroughly dug ourselves a hole big enough for a semi to drive through, do we realize the error of our ways and cry out for God's help.

Digging ourselves holes we must subsequently climb out of is a waste of the most precious resource we have been given in this life, time. Would not our time be better spent in prayer, than in attempting to undo what we, of our own volition, attempted to do in the first place? Would it not have been more productive for Joshua and the people to come before the Lord with prayer and supplication before going off to conquer Ai than wallowing in self-pity and doubt after having been defeated?

We learn from those who came before us so we don't make the same mistakes as they did. If we fail to learn, then we will tread the same ground, weep the same tears, and suffer the same heartaches. Nothing in life is more futile than making plans without consulting God, or making decisions without His counsel. If God is not in it, then no matter how much we toil, no matter how much we labor, no matter how much we sweat and bleed and ache, it will come to nothing.

It is the same for individuals as for entire nations. When both individuals and nations alike seek the counsel of God and obey His guidance, even the most difficult of tasks seem easy, and absent complications. When God is ignored, and His counsel is disregarded, the best laid plans crumble in on themselves, because His hand is not in it.

Examples are plentiful, both on a national scale, as well as individual ones, but I'm certain you have your own personal experiences to draw from in regards to the wisdom of obeying God in all things, and asking Him which way to turn. God is vexed when we do not take counsel with Him, and when we prefer the counsel of others over His.

Isaiah 30:1-2, "Woe to the rebellious children,' says the Lord, 'who take counsel, but not of Me, and who devise plans, but not of My Spirit, that they may add sin to sin; who walk to go down to Egypt and have not asked My advice, to strengthen themselves in the strength of Pharaoh, and to trust in the shadows of Egypt.'"

By now we ought to know that when we read the word 'woe' in the Bible, it is not a good thing. In fact, woe, means great sorrow and distress, misery, misfortune and calamity. So when God says 'woe to the rebellious children,' He means great sorrow, distress, misery, misfortune and calamity to the rebellious children.

Why? Why ought all these things to come upon them? These things ought to come upon them because they took counsel, but not of God, and devised plans, but not of God's Spirit. They found their strength not in God, but in the strength of Pharaoh and of Egypt, excluding God from their decision making process, walking to go down to Egypt of their own volition. God's people chose to trust in the visible strength of Pharaoh–which God would later tell His people would be their shame and their humiliation–rather than in His strength and providence.

God does not take being ignored, disobeyed, brushed aside, and slighted lightly. He doesn't just shrug His shoulders and say, 'well I would have preferred it if you'd come to Me, and taken counsel of Me, but I'll bless you anyway.'

'Woe to the rebellious children,' says the Lord. God sees taking counsel with another instead of Him, as rebellion. Whether we take counsel with ourselves, with our spouse, or with our friends and omit taking counsel with God, it is catalogued as rebellion. Taking this thread to its rightful conclusion–since rebellion is as the sin of witchcraft–what we are doing when we devise plans but not of God's Spirit and take counsel but not of Him, is practicing witchcraft.

'But Mike how can you say something so mean?'

Not I, but the Word of God said it–I just brought the idea to its rightful conclusion.

It is God's pleasure to commune, communicate, and fellowship with His creation. It is God's pleasure to do, as any good father would, and direct His children in the way they must go. To warn them of the pitfalls they ought to avoid, and remind them of the dangers lurking in the shadows throughout their journey. By the same token, it is God's displeasure to be ignored, disregarded and unheeded, all the more when we prefer the counsel and direction of another over Him. Not only was God upset with His people for not taking counsel with Him and devising plans by His Spirit, He was likewise upset because His people had chosen the counsel of Egypt and Pharaoh over His own.

One thing is certain. We cannot fault or blame God for our failures if we disregarded His counsel and disobeyed His commands to begin with. We cannot fault God for the shipwreck our life has become if we discounted His voice from the onset.

It was not God that led us to the edge of the precipice, and we know this because we never once asked God which road to take, or which task to undertake since beginning our journey. It is both futile and foolish to stand at the edge, stare off into the abyss, and blame God for our predicament when He had nothing whatsoever to do with it.

Many years ago, a friend of mine gave me a book for my birthday that outlined the habits of successful people. Since I read pretty much anything that's put in front of me, from shampoo bottles, to cereal boxes, to eighteen hundred page tomes written in the sixteenth century, I read the book within a couple nights. Still too young to understand or even appreciate what impact forming certain habits might have in life, I took the book more as an intellectual exercise than a roadmap to success or something worthy of emulating, and if you were to ask me today what the habits of successful people were I'd be hard pressed to remember them all.

One habit I endorse, something we ought to become as accustomed to doing as brushing our teeth in the morning, or turning off the lights when we leave the house, is taking counsel with God whenever we have to make a decision, or find ourselves at a crossroads. When asking God for His opinion and taking counsel with Him becomes habitual and common practice, we automatically eliminate the possibility of finding ourselves headed down the wrong path, or being outside His will.

All good things begin with prayer, and every failure begins with the lack thereof. When we pray is just as important as that we pray. It's not as though Joshua didn't pray at all. He did pray, he even tore his clothes, and put dust on his head, but this was after his army was defeated, after they fled from before the men of Ai, and after his men were slaughtered. Depending on the difficulty of the journey, and how much opposition we encounter, depending on how off script our plans have gone, eventually most individuals run to God, hoping that He salvage some of what they worked so hard for.

When God is our last resort, when we trust in the arm of the flesh and in our own prowess until we see no way out of the situation but to go before God, we are neither honoring God, nor do we trust in Him. To a certain extent, the old adage that there are no atheists in foxholes holds true, but as children of God we ought not to wait until we find ourselves in a foxhole to cry out to God. Rather, we must have a relationship and fellowship with Him throughout.

Yes, Joshua did pray. He prayed earnestly, and with tears, he tore his clothes and bowed before the presence of God, but only after the battle had been lost, and a handful of souls had overrun three thousand of his soldiers. Not only did Joshua pray, the elders of Israel prayed with him, fulfilling one of the prerequisites to corporate prayer, that of being united and as one when we approach God corporately.

Even so, the damage had already been done, the army had been put to flight, and in the words we see Joshua praying, we perceive a hint of doubt when it came to the purpose of God for His people. 'Alas, Lord God, why have You brought this people over the Jordan at all–to deliver us into the hand of the Amorites to destroy us?'

Joshua knew full well why God had brought the people over the Jordan, just as he knew that it was not to deliver them into the hand of the Amorites to be destroyed. Joshua was well aware of the promises of God to His people, he was well aware of where God was leading them, but it took one setback, one defeat to make even one such as Joshua murmur, and allow doubt to creep in.

Unfortunately Joshua was not unique when it came to murmuring during difficult situations. We see the selfsame predisposition for murmuring when times got tough in Moses, as well as the people of Israel as a whole. There are many worthwhile lessons in the Bible when it comes to the things we ought to do, and what we ought to practice, but there are also examples of what not to do, because the Bible was not selective when it came to the lives of the men it highlights.

One of the most refreshing things about the Bible is that it does not attempt to project an image of the men as something more than what they were, but reveals them to us honestly, openly, and with the requisite flaws. Joshua murmured, and the Word of God tells us he murmured. This was not overlooked, brushed under the rug, or dismissed. This episode in Joshua's life teaches us how not to approach God, as well as how not to address Him when certain situations arise.

The spirit in which we pray to God is as important as the timing of our prayer, and the fact that we pray.

We can pray in a spirit of rebellion, or in a spirit of criticism, which God will not receive as a sweet smelling sacrifice, because they're not. Weak faith produces discouragement; it produces criticism and murmuring whenever we happen upon a rough patch, or when our journey is not as easy as we expected it to be. It is one thing to ask God why, it is quite another to be argumentative with Him, and speak to Him as though He is at fault.

Joshua knew better, and still he spoke to God as though God had no reason for having allowed Israel to lose the battle against Ai. In His love, wisdom, patience, and longsuffering, God then proceeds to educate Joshua, and reveal to him the last reason why we oftentimes suffer defeats and setbacks, which also happened to be the reason Israel suffered defeat at the hands of a far smaller force.

Joshua 7:10-12, "So the Lord said to Joshua: 'Get up! Why do you lie thus on your face? Israel has sinned, and they have also transgressed My covenant which I commanded them. For they have even taken some of the accursed things, and have both stolen and deceived; and they have also put it among their own stuff. Therefore the children of Israel could not stand before their enemies, but turned their backs before their enemies, because they have become doomed to destruction. Neither will I be with you anymore, unless you destroy the accursed from among you.'"

Israel suffered defeat at the hands of Ai because they had sinned, and transgressed the covenant of God. God wasn't picking on Israel, He wasn't being mean, and He wasn't having a bad day. Israel had sinned, and God said He would neither be with the people or with Joshua himself anymore, unless the accursed was destroyed from among them.

One of the most obvious, yet simultaneously most overlooked lessons during this moment in Israel's history is the way in which God perceives sin. Admittedly, even much of Christendom has adopted the mantra 'if it's not hurting anyone else, it's none of my business,' but especially when it comes to the household of faith, and those who identify themselves as sons and daughters of God, the notion that your individual sin will not affect the entire camp is foolish and false on its face.

It was not as though half of Israel had sinned or transgressed. It was not as though half of Israel had taken some of the accursed things. One man named Achan committed a trespass regarding the accursed things, and now God tells Joshua that all the people had become doomed to destruction. Many a preacher today chooses not to preach against sin because they have talked themselves into believing that individual sin does not affect the body as a whole. What they have done, is talk themselves into believing a lie.

If we are all members of the same body, then with every member that is not performing optimally, with every member that is hurt, wounded, diseased or numb, the entire body suffers, and withers and loses vitality. The Word of God, both in the New and Old Testament, attempts to teach those who would follow after Christ the importance of individual sanctification, and the impact it has on the entire body. One man had sinned, and God was holding the entire nation responsible for it. One man had sinned, yet God said until such a time as the accursed thing was destroyed from among them, God would no longer be with His people.

Either the sin is removed from the camp, or the camp removes itself from the sin, but either way, God expects and even demands a clean, righteous, holy people, who place His will above their own, and His commandments above their desires.

It wasn't as though God had not made His will clear to His people. It was not as though they were ignorant concerning the accursed things or that they ought not to take them. This was not the first time God spoke to His people, it was not the first time He had warned them of the consequences of disobedience, but as is so often the case, the passing of time had dulled their memories, or they had chosen to disregard the Word and message of God altogether.

Deuteronomy 28:15, "But it shall come to pass, if you do not obey the voice of the Lord your God, to observe carefully all His commandments and His statutes which I command you today, that all these curses will come upon you and overtake you."

God had spoken. God had been explicit. God had warned of what would happen if they did not obey his voice and carefully observe all His commandments. Among the many things God listed as consequence to their disobedience, we also find what happened when the three thousand went up to defeat Ai.

Deuteronomy 28:25, "The Lord will cause you to be defeated before your enemies; you shall go out one way against them and flee seven ways before them; and you shall become troublesome to all the kingdoms of the earth."

Two ways are set before every man: the way of obedience or the way of rebellion. Each man, and nation chooses the way they will follow, and either reap the reward of their obedience, or suffer the consequences of their rebellion. In His love God warns. In His love God instructs. In His love God shows us the outcome of our rebellion vividly, and without reservation, yet in our hard-heartedness, we still choose the way of rebellion thinking we know better, and that we will succeed where others have failed, because we are wiser than our predecessors.

Obedience to God makes us victorious even when we are one against a thousand. Disobedience and rebellion cause our defeat even before the first blow is struck. In reading the passage in Deuteronomy, one can't help but notice that defeat will not come because your enemies are better equipped, have the high ground, are more experienced soldiers, or are greater in number, but rather the Lord will cause the defeat.

It might seem harsh to some, seeing that the Lord Himself will cause defeat when we are disobedient, but the takeaway lesson in this is how unacceptable disobedience and rebellion are seen of God, not how harsh God can be. God's love, mercy, peace and goodness are extended to all who obey, to all who bow before Him and worship Him. He keeps those who are His, He protects them, and He guides them, and gives them victory even when victory is unexpected. To live with the expectation of God's providence while being in active, open, and ongoing rebellion against Him, is not only foolish but illogical and absent reason. We cannot do what God abhors, shake our fist toward heaven, pretend He does not exist, and still, somehow demand He bless us, keep us, and give us victory.

Suffering defeat is a consequence of disobedience. Whether individually or as a nation, when we are in obedience toward God we are under His protection. When we choose the way of disobedience however, God's hand is removed and our enemies encamp around us unhindered. God made both paths clear to His people. He told them what would become of them if they chose rebellion and disobedience, but He also told them what their lot would be if they chose to obey.

Deuteronomy 28:2, "All these blessings shall come upon you and overtake you, because you obey the voice of the Lord your God."

Deuteronomy 28:7, "The Lord will cause your enemies who rise against you to be defeated before your face; they shall come out against you one way and flee before you seven ways."

Because you obey the voice of the Lord, He will cause your enemies who rise against you to be defeated before your face. This is the promise of God, contingent on whether or not obedience was a reality in the lives of the people. The people knew both the goodness and the severity of God, and though they knew His warnings as well as His promises, one among them chose to disregard God's command, and take for himself the unclean and accursed thing.

Sin metastasizes. If allowed to thrive unchecked, sin will invariably develop secondary malignant growths, spreading out from the primary site, and destroying everything in its path. We, as children of God, are not doing anyone any favors by treating sin with kid gloves, or by doing our utmost not to challenge those openly living in sin to repentance. Some just can't be bothered to get out of their comfort zones, others are inhibited by cowardice, and others still don't think sin is such a big issue that it has to be confronted in the church. Because these mentalities are prevalent within the household of faith, sin is running rampant and where there was one in rebellion, there are now four, and where there are four there will soon be eight.

Sin is not content with being static. Sin grows, it multiplies, it infects, because its sole purpose is the destruction of the house of God, and it does not rest until it has reached its objective.

The sin of one man had spread, and it now affected the entire nation.

It takes some doing to wrap our minds around the fact that one singular solitary sin, caused an entire nation to grow discouraged, and fearful of its enemies, to spurn the wrath of God, and see themselves defeated in a most complete and undeniable way.

The sin may be singular, but the consequences of that singular sin are multiple. One sin caused defeat, discouragement, fear, the wrath of God, the absence of God's presence, and God's rejection of Joshua's prayer. After Joshua's heartfelt plea, after he tore his clothes and put dust on his head, God's answer was, 'get up! Israel has sinned, and they have also transgressed.' Before God could answer Joshua's prayer, the sin had to be removed from among the people, and the people had to be sanctified.

Sin keeps prayer from being answered. No, Joshua had not committed trespass, Joshua had not sinned, but one who was under his authority had, and God held the entire nation responsible. Until that one individual was dealt with, until the accursed was destroyed from among the people, God vowed not to be with His people anymore.

How serious is sin in the sight of God? Serious enough to reject the prayer of His faithful servant Joshua until the sin was dealt with. If God rejected the prayer of Joshua for a sin someone else committed, what makes us think He will not reject our prayers when we ourselves willfully persist in our sins without repentance or contrition?

This is one of the reasons why the doctrines which insist that you need not stop sinning, you need not repent, you need not amend your ways, but simply raise a limp-wristed hand in a church service are so dangerous. Because individuals are never told they must repent, they never do, and because they continue in their sin their prayers are never answered. Because the individuals in question never receive an answer to their prayers, because they never know true intimacy with God due to the sin that stands as a wall between Him and them, they grow disenchanted with the faith, bored even, and leave God in their rear view looking for more exciting and stimulating experiences.

Repentance must be preached within the household of faith, for only when we have put away the accursed things from among us, will God answer our prayers, and give us victory. In order to put away the accursed thing from among us, we must first identify it, isolate it, and then remove it from within the congregation. If an individual refuses repentance, then that individual has no desire to live for God, or be obedient to God, but rather they want the assurance of salvation while living whichever way they please.

As tempting as this path might be for many, beware, God is not mocked and what a man sows a man will surely reap. We cannot sow rebellion, disobedience, habitual sin and indifference toward the Word of God, and reap eternity with Him in paradise. It matters not how many individuals tell you otherwise, first you have the Scriptures to contend with, then reason itself invalidates such a ludicrous premise. You belong to the one you serve, the one you've given your heart to, and the one you spend your time with. Since no man can serve two masters, each one of us is either committed wholeheartedly to God, living in obedience of Him, and worshipping Him alone, or to Satan, living in rebellion towards righteousness and following after the desires of the flesh.

It is that simple; that black and white; that cut-and-dried.

In God's estimation Israel sinned, even though only Achan committed a trespass regarding the accursed things. God saw His people as a whole, and the trespass of one, as the trespass of all.

Ecclesiastes 9:18, "Wisdom is better than weapons of war; but one sinner destroys much good."

One man sinned, but through Achan's disobedience the whole of God's people was seen as impure. There are consequences to sin beyond the individual, especially when that individual belongs to a body, and is counted among its members. Although some are quick to point to the Old Testament and say 'different times, different rules,' the notion that sin within the body compromises the entire body, is found in the New Testament as well.

1 Corinthians 5:11-13, "But now I have written to you not to keep company with anyone named a brother, who is a fornicator, or covetous, or an idolater, or a reviler, or a drunkard, or an extortioner — not even to eat with such a person. For what have I to do with judging those also who are outside? Do you not judge those who are inside? But those who are outside God judges. Therefore 'put away from yourselves that wicked person.'"

Within the framework of this passage we understand that spiritually speaking, God sees those who are on the inside, and those who are on the outside. God judges those who are on the outside; God judges those who are of the world. What the Bible tells us we are not to keep company with, is anyone named a brother who continues in their sin, be they a fornicator, covetous, an idolater, a drunkard or a reviler. It is not speaking of those of the world whom it is our duty to preach Christ to, it is speaking of individuals calling themselves brothers in Christ, living like the world they are supposed to have been unshackled from.

Our duty as children of God is to make certain that those who are on the inside walk the straight and narrow path of faith, being obedient to God, and bringing glory and honor to His name. We are accountable to each other as members of the Body of Christ, and as such ought to not only rebuke in love when necessary, but be a shoulder to lean on when the road gets hard. With what the church has become, or what it has been redefined as, it is difficult to understand the beauty of the interconnectedness Jesus intended His church to be in. Both in the spiritual, as well as in the physical our duty is to be there for each other, feel with each other, and carry each other if need be.

Having grown up in a communist country where at any given moment half the men in our congregation were being tortured, imprisoned, or sent off to labor camps, it was easy to see the interconnectedness I speak of in action. If a brother was in jail, the rest of the church pitched in and helped his family however they could, from bringing groceries, to doing farm chores, to giving counsel to their children if the need arose.

In their hearts and minds, in word and in deed, they were one body, and they understood that if one member of the body suffers, the rest of the body will suffer as well.

One man had brought dishonor to the entire nation, just as by their actions, certain individuals bring shame to the household of faith today. The essence of Achan's guilt was that he had taken an accursed thing into his house. Is there something inherently wrong with silver, gold, or garments, since these are the things Achan took and hid in his tent? No, there is nothing inherently wrong with these things, but they became accursed the moment God commanded that such things not be taken by any of the Israelites.

We know what God calls sin. We know what God calls accursed. His Word is explicit in regards to what He deems as sinful, what He deems as a trespass or transgression. There is no getting around the Word of God, there is no denying the veracity thereof, and we will suffer the selfsame defeats as Israel did, until these things are removed from our midst.

Joshua 7:13, "Get up, sanctify the people, and say, 'sanctify yourselves for tomorrow, because thus says the Lord God of Israel: 'There is an accursed thing in your midst, O Israel; you cannot stand before your enemies until you take away the accursed thing from among you.'"

Until the people were sanctified, and until the accursed thing was removed from among them, God would not hear the prayer of Joshua. Not only would God not hear the prayer of Joshua until these things were done, Israel would not be able to stand before its enemies either.

It goes without saying God loved Joshua. It was God after all, who handpicked Joshua to take the place of Moses as leader of God's people, but God cannot overlook sin even among those He loves, or better still, especially among those He loves. He is a holy God, He is a righteous God, and His love in no way nullifies or abolishes His holiness and righteousness.

Because He loves He chastens, for He chastens those He loves, and because we love Him in kind we are obedient toward His voice, and do as commanded sanctifying ourselves and putting away the accursed thing from among us. God can be both holy and loving, both righteous and merciful, because His nature is not isolated to one attribute. He isn't just love, He isn't just mercy, He isn't just holiness or righteousness…He is all these things, not just one of these things.

It was only when the sin was dealt with that God gave victory to Israel once more. It was only when the accursed thing was removed from the camp that God heard the prayers of Joshua, and continued to give him victory, even against enemies much more imposing than the citizenry of Ai.

THE PRAYER OF SAMSON

Ask ten different people what they know of Samson and chances are you will get ten different answers. Perhaps some will say he was a judge, but more likely you will be regaled with stories of his strength, and reminded that he killed a thousand men with a jawbone.

Although all these things are true of Samson–he was a judge, and he did kill a thousand Philistines with a jawbone–he was also a child of promise, foretold of by an angel, whose mother was given very specific instructions as to how he ought to be brought up, and what he would become.

Even with his many flaws, and woefully self-destructive decisions, Samson was still a man who had faith in God, to the extent that even the author of Hebrews mentions him among such notables as Enoch, Abraham, Moses, Gideon, Isaac, David and Samuel. It is no small feat to be mentioned in the same breath as such heroes of the faith, yet here, Samson is mentioned among them nonetheless.

Samson was a judge among the people of God. A man chosen of God from before his birth to be a Nazirite to God, meaning one who is consecrated, separated, or holy unto God. The Nazirites were those who voluntarily took a vow of abstinence from wine, refrained from cutting their hair, and did not become impure by coming in contact with corpses or graves.

The angel of the Lord spoke to Samson's mother, informing her that he would be one such Nazirite, a man consecrated unto God.

Judges 13:4, "For behold, you shall conceive and bear a son. And no razor shall come upon his head, for the child shall be a Nazirite to God from the womb; he shall begin to deliver Israel out of the hand of the Philistines."

Although the life of Samson teaches us many things, one of the most practical things it teaches us is that potential can be, and often is, readily wasted. Just because someone has potential and is even foretold of by an angel of the Lord, it does not mean that they will live up to it or even do their duty before God, as Samson so clearly shows us.

It is always more tragic to see a life brimming with potential being thoroughly wasted than to see an average or less than average individual not striving to excel. The angel of the Lord specifically told Samson's parents that he was to do a great work for God by delivering Israel out of the hand of the Philistines. He confirmed this time and again, and in order to help Samson accomplish this task, God would even give him supernatural physical strength. Anyone who is even tangentially familiar with the story of Samson knows that rather than fulfill God's plan, Samson grew up to waste his strength by fulfilling his own lusts, desires, and penchants.

At the end of his twenty years of judgeship, Delilah, a harlot, finally convinces Samson to part with his long held secret, and reveal the source of his strength, his long hair. Although a discussion concerning the secret of Samson's strength not being his hair, but rather his unique relationship with God as symbolized in his pledge not to cut his hair would be a fascinating one indeed, we will table that particular discussion for now and focus on the prayer of Samson instead.

The prayer of Samson we will be discussing comes near the end of his life. His prayer comes as he is surrounded by his enemies, defeated, blinded, and made to be a grinder in the prison. Here was a man who was judge over the people of God, who had the power of God coursing through him to such an extent that thousands of years later he is still known as the strongest man to ever live, yet he threw it all away for the passing pleasures of this present life.

The life of Samson is a tragic one. It is a life worthy of contemplation because his personal failures led him to the point of causing God to take away his power, having his eyes put out, and being made to perform for the Philistines. Even during the last moments of his life however, Samson still found the wherewithal to cry out to God, praying a prayer very different from the prayers of Jesus or Stephen of the New Testament. The prayer of Samson was not conciliatory in nature, he did not ask God to forgive the Philistines for what they had done, but rather for the strength to take vengeance on the Philistines who had taken his eyes.

What is more interesting than the prayer itself, is the fact that God answered it, and though we will be discussing the prayer of Samson and the context thereof, we will also be discussing why God would answer a prayer of vengeance and revenge.

One thing is certain: God does as He wills, and in our attempt to understand certain actions God takes, this must perpetually be at the forefront of our minds. Although God Himself said vengeance is His, here we have a man who having lost his way, comes before God once more and asks for the strength to take vengeance upon the Philistines, and God answers his prayer granting him the strength to do just that.

We can never fail to understand that there are exceptions to certain rules within the Word of God, but these exceptions are not made by men, but by God Himself. Why God makes certain exceptions at certain times, is something known only to Him, but we can try to glean and understand the nature of a situation, and what led to a certain action God took, based on Scripture and the entire context of the situation as it stands.

Judges 16:28, "Then Samson called to the Lord, saying, 'O Lord God, remember me, I pray! Strengthen me, I pray, just this once, O God, that I may with one blow take vengeance on the Philistines for my two eyes!'"

Minutes after uttering this prayer, Samson would be dead, along with three thousand Philistines. Samson knew his time was at hand...of this he had no doubt. Yet, there was no prayer for forgiveness in regards to the Philistines and what they had done, but rather a prayer of vengeance, for God to remember him, and strengthen him once more that he might deal justly with the Philistines for his two eyes. Having the distinct honor of never whitewashing individuals, or airbrushing their wrinkles, the Word of God presents Samson to us in his true light, revealing his unequaled strength, and speaking of his exploits, but also revealing his weaknesses, and what his weaknesses led him to.

Samson was a man of controversial character. Although he is lauded by many, even admired by some, he continues to be misunderstood to this day. One thing is certain; Samson was chosen of God and destined for a great plan. Seeing as this is the case, and it is irrefutable that God chose Samson and destined him, the question which begs to be asked, is: did God fail? Did God make a mistake in choosing Samson as judge?

No, God did not fail. No, God did not make a mistake, because God does not make mistakes. There was, however, the element of human choice in this entire scenario, and though God might have a plan, though God might choose an individual for a specific task and purpose, the individual can still stray, the individual can still refuse God, becoming disobedient and even rebellious to the voice and unction of the Lord.

We are not automatons. We are not preprogrammed robots who have no choice in whether or not we obey, serve, or fulfill our duties before God. We have choice, and will, and God would have it no other way, for His desire is that we serve out of love, not because He compelled us or forced us to do it. The next time you hear another individual say that man has no say in whether or not he serves God, and or that man is utterly incapable of choosing between right or wrong, point him to Samson, to what the angel of the Lord had testified of him and his life before he was even born, and then to the life he lived, more in rebellion of God than in obedience of Him.

God has a plan and a purpose for each of us. He has a calling to which He has called us as individuals, but whether we walk in our calling, or obey the unction of the Lord is entirely up to us. Yes, I know the notion of personal accountability is a bitter pill for many. We would rather believe we have no choice in whether we follow after Christ or not, than believe we are accountable for our choices, and that our rebellion toward Him was a choice on our part.

When we come to believe we are not accountable for any of the choices we make because our existence has already been predestined, and no matter what we do we cannot follow after Christ if it was not so foreordained, then, when we stumble, fall, and don't get up again, we just shrug our shoulders and think to ourselves that perhaps we were not among the chosen to begin with.

Believing that man can no more accept or reject God on his own than he could reconfigure the stars in the heavens, takes away from man's personal responsibility and accountability toward God. Grace is offered freely; man must receive it. Samson was supposed to begin delivering Israel out of the hand of the Philistines, and he ended up being delivered into the hands of the Philistines who made sport of him. God's plan for Samson was different than the outcome of his existence, but Samson chose rebellion rather than obedience with consistency, and drew further away from God with each subsequent act of rebellion.

Destined for greatness, destined to be the instrument of God's salvation in regards to His people, Samson ends up dying along with the lawless, the Philistines, those who served other gods and worshiped idols.

Samson did not start out as rebellious. He did not start out doing that which God had commanded him not to do. His descent, as most descents are, was gradual, and one thing led to another until Samson surrendered his heart to sin. Samson began as one blessed of God. He ended up as one whom the Philistines mocked and ridiculed.

Judges 13:24, "So the woman bore a son and called his name Samson; and the child grew, and the Lord blessed him."

Samson wasn't blessed in the temple, by a preacher, by a priest, or by a pastor. The Lord blessed Samson, and the Spirit of the Lord began to move upon him. From early youth, Samson had everything going for him. He enjoyed every benefit one can enjoy from the hand of God, from being blessed of the Lord, to having the Spirit of the Lord move upon him. Yet, something happened along the way the man Samson became, and the man he was supposed to have been, were two very different individuals.

We realize Samson was special, because of certain things highlighted in his biography. One of the most telling signs that Samson was special is that the Spirit of the Lord moved upon him. Since Pentecost the spirit of the Lord moves upon all the servants of the Lord. Before Pentecost it was not so. In the days of old, during the time of Samson, and up until the advent of the Holy Spirit, the

Spirit of the Lord moved only upon those with a special calling, or those called to a higher calling.

The judges of Samson's day were such individuals. They were called of God to a greater calling than the contemporaries of their day, and we see other judges during the same time period being imbued with the Spirit of the Lord that they might carry out the duties assigned to them. Although Samson was not alone in having the Spirit of the Lord move upon him–as within the same book of the Bible we see both Othniel, the first of the biblical judges, as well as Gideon being endowed with the selfsame Spirit–the supernatural physical strength he exhibited was unique to Samson in the entirety of Scripture.

Samson was a man upon whom the Spirit of the Lord moved. The exploits Samson did, the physical strength he exhibited, were not of him. They were not due to his pedigree or genetics, they were due to the power of God residing in him, and working through him. It is a glorious thing to be led by the Spirit of the Lord and to have the Spirit of the Lord move upon us, but it becomes dangerous and oftentimes destructive when we begin to see what the Spirit does as our doing, our exploits, and our accomplishments. When we start to believe we are doing it on our own, rather than the Spirit working through us, we begin to take the work of God for granted, as well as the gifting with which we have been endowed.

Samson was strong because God made him strong. Somewhere along the way Samson forgot this simple truth, and paid a dear price for it. Not only was Samson blessed of the Lord, not only did the Spirit of the Lord move upon him, he knew he had been set apart as a Nazirite unto God since before his birth. Samson lived with the awareness of what had been invested in him. He lived with the awareness of the great and high calling he had been called to.

Judges 16:16-17, "And it came to pass, when she pestered him daily with her words and pressed him, so that his soul was vexed to death, that he told her all his heart, and said to her, 'No razor has ever come upon my head, for I have been a Nazirite to God from my mother's womb. If I am shaven, then my strength will leave me, and I shall become weak, and be like any other man.'"

Samson knew he had been set apart as unto God, and he also knew the consequences of having his head shaven. Samson knew he would be like any other man if his head were ever to be shaved. We know the consequence of rebellion, and we know the consequence of disobedience. We are not blind as to what will occur if we do contrary to the Word and will of God. Even so, more often than we would like to admit, we choose disobedience and rebellion as Samson did.

How does one who is chosen of God, and knows he is chosen of God, come to pray to God in a pagan temple, blind, and surrounded by his enemies? What leads a man who had all the potential in the world, all the strength he would ever need, the highest position in the land, and the inherent capacity to do good, to throw it all away for momentary pleasure and worldly lusts?

It is important to know what led to Samson's downfall, because any one of us is susceptible if we are not watchful, prayerful and obedient toward God. Any man or woman walking the earth today is susceptible to temptation if they have not learned to resist temptation, and resist the devil himself that he might flee. Very rarely does one single, solitary thing lead to the downfall of an individual. More often than not, it is an amalgam of little things, small steps, which eventually leads one over the edge of the precipice altogether.

The first step Samson took toward his downfall is that he started to flirt with sin. For Samson, sin was not a dangerous thing, it was not a destructive thing, it was something he flirted with, and mocked at, until it eventually destroyed him.

Proverbs 14:9, "Fools mock at sin, but among the upright there is favor."

As so many do today, Samson underestimated the power and danger of sin. He did not see sin for what it was, but rather, Samson saw sin as how sin chose to present itself. Sin never reveals its true face; it is far too hideous for any man to embrace it. Sin camouflages its true nature; it camouflages its true intent, focusing on the momentary pleasure itself, rather than the inevitable lifelong ramifications and consequences of the momentary pleasure.

When we disregard the warnings of God throughout the Scriptures concerning the danger of sin, we are doing ourselves a disservice, while simultaneously inferring that God somehow exaggerated or didn't really know what He was talking about. God speaks of sin in the Scripture admonishing us to flee the very appearance of evil, because He knows how much of a sway sin will have over the heart of man if it is allowed to fester and take root therein. God knows how completely and utterly sin destroys. He knows how it befouls every heart it resides in, and in love, He warns repeatedly that as children of the light and pursuers of righteousness, we must break ties with sin altogether.

Although Samson knew better, he did not heed the warnings of God, he did not treat sin with the seriousness with which sin ought to be treated, and his ongoing flirtation with sin led to something infinitely more damaging…something even the strength of the strongest man to ever live could not overcome.

Do we view sin as God views sin? Do we view sin as a dangerous, destructive force, or do we view sin the way sin tries to present itself as a harmless dalliance? We have seen the scattered remains sin has left in its wake. We have seen the broken homes, the ruined lives, the premature deaths, and yet, many still choose to flirt with sin as Samson did, treating it lightly.

The second step in Samson's downfall was allowing himself to be drawn toward, or attracted to the forbidden things.

Judges 14:1-3, "Now Samson went down to Timnah, and saw a woman in Timnah of the daughters of the Philistines. So he went up and told his father and mother, saying, 'I have seen a woman in Timnah of the daughters of the Philistines; now therefore, get her for me as a wife.' Then his father and mother said to him, 'is there no woman among the daughters of your brethren, or among all my people, that you must go and get a wife from the uncircumcised Philistines?' And Samson said to his father, 'get her for me, for she pleases me well.'"

So what was wrong in this? Samson was just following his heart, he had seen a girl, she was pleasing to the eye, and wanted to marry her. On the surface, it seemed like a love story. Many today would applaud Samson for thinking outside the box, for taking the initiative, and for not being swayed from love by the disapproval of his parents.

When digging deeper, however, we come to realize that the Philistines, the people from which the girl who well pleased Samson came, were idol worshippers of the worst kind, and sworn enemies of the people of God. Samson's only criterion was that the girl pleased him well, focusing on the momentary pleasure of beauty, instead of obedience to the will of God in regards to co-mingling with idol worshippers.

Deuteronomy 7:3-5, "Nor shall you make marriages with them. You shall not give your daughters to their son, nor take their daughter for your son. For they will turn your sons away from following Me, to serve other gods; so the anger of the Lord will be aroused against you and destroy you suddenly."

Samson knew the law of God. He knew the commandments of God, and he chose to disregard them. In every act of rebellion, in every act of disobedience, in every sin, there is a dose of pleasure. The Philistine Samson had chosen, the woman he wanted as a wife pleased him well, and for no other reason than that she pleased him well, he wanted her for a wife.

Because Samson opened the door, the enemy came in, and from seeing a Philistine who was pleasing to his eye, he sees another, who happened to be a harlot, and this time does more than look.

Judges 16:1, 'Then Samson went to Gaza and saw a harlot there, and went in to her."

From allowing for the possibility of taking a Philistine for a wife, Samson has now fallen to the low of being with a woman of ill repute. Samson's entourage also contributed to his downfall. Instead of surrounding himself with men of God, he surrounded himself with revelers and partiers whose only desire was to see the continuation of their good time.

Judges 14:10-11, "So his father went down to the woman. And Samson gave a feast there, for young men used to do so. And it was so, when they saw him, that they brought thirty companions to be with him."

It was not the custom of the Jews to give a feast, it was the custom of the Philistines, and Samson has started to follow their customs in the giving of the feast. The celebration lasted for seven days, and the man who was consecrated unto God, the man sworn never to touch alcohol, or even anything that might be construed as alcohol, imbibed and reveled along with the thirty companions that had been brought to be with him.

We have also been consecrated unto God. We have also been set apart, sanctified and made holy unto Him. When we choose disobedience and rebellion over humility and subservience, we are doing what Samson did, with the full knowledge that it displeases God. Somewhere near the last moments of Samson's downfall, he also opened his heart to those he ought to have kept it hidden from. Placing our trust in the wrong individuals can be catastrophic and have lasting repercussions. Samson told Delilah all his heart, and because of this the Philistines knew the one secret that could undo him.

Micah 7:5, "Do not trust in a friend; Do not put your confidence in a companion; Guard the doors of your mouth from her who lies in your bosom."

Because Samson did not guard his heart, because he did not heed the warnings of God, because he disregarded the commandments of God, he finds himself impotent, powerless, without the ability to defend himself against the Philistines. It used to be so easy for him. It used to take almost no effort for Samson to defeat entire regiments of Philistines, but now that he had revealed his heart and had subsequently been betrayed, what was once easy, and requiring little effort, now became impossible.

We take for granted the presence of God in our lives. We take for granted our ability to overcome certain obstacles, until God is no longer there. Until His strength no longer goes before us, and only then do we realize the true measure of our impotence. Samson believed himself capable of overcoming the Philistines even after his hair was shaved off. Even after he had trampled upon his covenant with God, Samson expected to shake himself free as at other times, only to discover that the Lord had departed from him.

All the strength Samson perceived as his own, all the power and the ability he had believed were at his whim, disappeared in an instant when the Lord was no longer present.

Judges 16:20, "And she said, 'The Philistines are upon you, Samson!' So he awoke from his sleep, and said, 'I will go out as before, at other times, and shake myself free!' But he did not know that the Lord had departed from him."

After all he had done, Samson still assumed the Lord would be with him. One of the reasons we must continually bring to remembrance all that Jesus has done for us, is so that it remains fresh on our minds, and constant in our awareness. We can never perceive what Jesus did on the cross as something usual or ordinary, because once we do, we begin to take His presence in our lives for granted, and assume as Samson did, that He will always be with us regardless of what we do.

Although Samson knew he had been consecrated to God, and knew God had endowed him with special power, what he lost sight of along the way is that God can take away just as readily as He gives. Rather than have the understanding of Job, and say 'the Lord gives and the Lord takes away,' many today have presumed, without any Biblical foundation, that the Lord simply gives, and gives, without ever taking away, no matter the reason or cause. The Lord not only gives, the Lord also takes away. When we are not faithful in the little we've been given, He takes it away and gives it to another who will be.

'What about the gifts of God being without repentance? How can God depart from one such as Samson in one breath, and then say His gifts are without repentance?'

In order to understand how both can be true, we must understand what the word repentance means. Repentance means regret, sorrow, or remorse, and yes, the gifts of God are without repentance. He is not sorry for having called or gifted someone; He does not feel sorrow or remorse for having endowed an individual with special gifting. By the same token, He cannot allow His gifting to reside in a heart that has willingly given itself over to rebellion and lawlessness. If this was the case, then He would not be the righteous, holy God, before whom nothing wicked or defiled can stand. Without repentance does not mean irrevocable, it just means God is not sorry for having done it!

Samson is not the only individual from whom the Lord departed in the Bible. Saul, the first king of Israel, also had the Spirit of the Lord depart from him, and the Spirit of the Lord was replaced by a distressing spirit which troubled him. Both Samson and Saul disobeyed and rebelled against the commands of the Lord, and as the consequence of their disobedience the Lord departed from them. What could be more horrible than thinking the Lord is with you, when in fact He has long departed?

I cringe when I counsel individuals, and their excuse for not repenting, and continuing in their habitual sin is that they feel the Lord is still with them. Samson felt the Lord was still with him, until he discovered otherwise. You cannot live in sin, circumvent repentance, speak, live, act, and do as the world does, and expect the Lord to be with you. In many a life, the Lord has long departed, and they haven't even noticed.

> *2 Chronicles 15:1-2, "Now the Spirit of God came upon Azariah the son of Oded. And he went out to meet Asa, and said to him: 'Hear me, Asa, and all Judah and Benjamin. The Lord is with you while you are with Him. If you seek Him, He will be found by you; but if you forsake Him, He will forsake you.'"*

The Spirit of the Lord had come upon Azariah, and what he was doing, was prophesying, speaking a message from God to Asa, all of Judah, and Benjamin. The message was simple, straightforward, and is highly controversial in our day and age.
'The Lord is with you while you are with Him.'

'But that can't be…nope, don't believe it. I raised my hand in church, and the pastor said I didn't have to do anything whatsoever after that, 'cause if I tried to live different than before it would be works and stuff.'

Although a large percentage of the church today might discount the Scripture passages that speak of striving to enter through the narrow gate, repentance, holiness unto God, and other unpopular and circumvented doctrines of the faith, they are, nevertheless, still in the Book, a perpetual thorn in the side of those who insist that raising a limp-wristed hand in a church service gets us a one way ticket to Paradise.

'If you seek Him, He will be found by you; but if you forsake Him, He will forsake you.'

Tragically, the church has long distanced itself from the notion of reciprocity when it comes to a relationship with God. For the past few decades we have been taught that God will essentially kidnap us, and force us to love Him, even if our hearts continue to be in a state of rebellion, consistently choosing to ignore His Word. Love is reciprocal, and reciprocity is essential in any relationship. Yes, He first loved us. This He proved on the cross beyond doubt, but we must also love Him if we desire a relationship with Him. If we seek Him, He will be found. He is with us while we are with Him, but if we forsake Him, He will forsake us.

Samson forsook God, and God departed from Samson. After giving Samson multiple opportunities to repent, after allowing him to see the error of his way in the hopes that he would return to the path for which he had been consecrated, the Lord departed, and Samson lost his strength.

From being a man blessed of God, Samson becomes a man from whom the Lord departed. From seeing the power of the Lord coursing through him, Samson is now as impotent as any other man as the Philistines take him, put out his eyes, and bring him down to Gaza.

There is only pain, sorrow, loss, and hurt in rebellion. No good can come of forsaking God, no good can come of ignoring His commandments, and every man who has attempted to do so, has seen the folly of his way only when it was too late. Belatedly, all those who take the grace of Christ for granted, and who take lightly what He did on the cross come to realize the foolishness of their way. One day, as we stand before He who was, and is, and always shall be, even the most ardent of atheists will know He lives. They will look upon the One they mocked, and ridiculed, the one they denied and blasphemed, but they will not be able to remedy their rebellion, nor will they have another occasion to repent of their lawlessness.

Tragic as the unfolding of Samson's life may seem to us, in the end, he did have an opportunity for repentance. He did have an opportunity to cry out to God, something that many simply don't get as they put off having a relationship with God until it's too late. There is no doubt in that Samson dealt treacherously with God, and as such he was ashamed, and brought low.

When we compare Samson's actions and David's actions in regards to one's enemies, we see the difference in temperament as well as approach. While Samson trusted in himself, and went to confront the Philistines on his own, thinking it would be as before, David waited on the Lord to deal with his enemies.

Psalm 25:1-3, "To You, O Lord, I lift up my soul. O my God, I trust in You; Let me not be ashamed; Let not my enemies triumph over me. Indeed, let no one who waits on You be ashamed; Let those be ashamed who deal treacherously without cause."

Even with the extent of Samson's fall from grace, even with the Lord having departed from him, God still extended grace to him, attempting to remind him of all he'd lost, and bring him back to a state of repentance. God was attempting to wake Samson up through his imprisonment and the taking of his eyesight, so he might remember from whence he had fallen. During an individual's descent into rebellion it is very difficult for them to see from whence they fell. Their entire focus and purpose is to descend ever deeper, until they reach the bottom. Once they've reached the bottom, they can retrace their steps, look back up, and see just how far into the pit they'd descended.

Samson had reached the bottom. The Philistines had already taken his dignity, they'd already taken his pride, they had shaved his head and put out his eyes, and the only thing left to do, that would be as a mercy to Samson, was to take his life.

It was at this low point, at the absolute bottom, that God once more tries to awaken him to the reality of his rebellion, disobedience, and transgression in the hope that he might repent. If we don't make time for God in our freedom, the situation will most likely arise when God will be all we have time for. Whether in a

Philistine cell, or in the belly of a fish, God finds ways of humbling us, and bringing our focus back on Him.

Up until the moment he got swallowed by the fish, Jonah was busy doing other things, like running away from God. In the belly of the fish however, Jonah wasn't distracted by other things, he wasn't trying to hatch other plans, or find an escape route, so from the depths, he cried out to God, and God heard him. Why must it take prison, or the belly of a fish for some to cry out to God?

It is easier to live in obedience of God, than suffer the consequences of rebellion. It is easier to maintain a relationship with God during the good times, than grope about for Him in our desperation. When we maintain relationship with God we know where He is, and He knows where we are at all times. Not a second will go by wherein He will not be standing beside us, guiding us, keeping us, and protecting us.

When we allow distractions to dictate our actions, when we allow rebellion to take root in our heart, when we disobey God even though we know better, then God will depart seeing as He is not wanted, and being the gentleman that He is, God doesn't stay where He isn't welcome. Anything we place before God in our hearts is an idol, and God will not abide it. If God and He alone is not on the throne of the heart, then whatever else is there—whether our possessions, our position, our spouse, or our children—is our surrogate God.

Often times, if we are honest with ourselves, we will be stunned to discover the self, sitting merrily where only God should reside. The pride of flesh is a tricky enemy, one who knows our weaknesses and exploits them with every opportunity. If we allow ourselves to be swayed by the honey pride pours into our ear, we will find ourselves facing our enemy alone, for God has long departed. When we keep God in our hearts, when we live in obedience to Him, and in remembrance of what Jesus did, then we will not run the risk of allowing idols to invade our heart, nor will we willfully usurp His throne and give it to another.

In all things, the preeminence of God must be evident and visible, and then all will know we are His children, and He is our Father. There are moments in our life when God attempts to awaken us. He sees us beginning to stray, He sees us beginning to subvert His authority, He sees us beginning to give our heart over to another, and in His love and mercy He stirs us in the hope of awakening us.

It was in Samson's isolation and suffering that God attempted to awaken him. Lest we forget, Samson had his eyes put out, and it wasn't in an operating room, or with anesthesia. Samson was now a regular, everyday human being, and the Philistines put out his eyes. Whether with a sword, a knife or a stick we don't know, but what we can be certain of is that Samson was suffering. His dignity was likewise taken from him as this once feared man, this judge of the people of Israel was now made to be a grinder in a prison.

Samson's days and nights were now restricted to contemplating how far he'd fallen, sitting in a prison cell, and grinding at the mill like an ox, or a beast of burden. God would never make us grind at the mill, but the enemy surely would. When we abandon God, and forsake Him thinking the grass is greener on the other side, it's only a matter of time before we realize how much we took for granted while working for God.

God is not a cruel taskmaster, but the devil is, and Samson was finding this out firsthand. It was here, when all hope had abandoned him, when what he had once been was a long ago memory, that Samson begins to cry out to God.

Judges 16:28, "Then Samson called to the Lord, saying, 'O Lord God, remember me, I pray! Strengthen me, I pray, just this once, O God, that I may with one blow take vengeance on the Philistines for my two eyes!'"

God hears when we call out to Him. Possessing this knowledge, knowing with certainty that He hears when we cry out, is one of the most comforting things for us as children of God. God is never busy, He is never out of reach, and He is never distracted by something else. Whenever you call on Him, He will hear. Samson called out to God in the midst of his despair. Here he was, once great, now made to perform for the Philistines, who gave the credit for Samson's capture to their god Dagon. This once proud man, this man for whom nothing seemed impossible, now humbles himself, he capitulates, and realizes he can't do it on his own. Samson became aware of his own impotence, and in humility cried out to God to strengthen Him once more.

Samson is one of those biblical figures we can all relate to in greater or lesser fashion, because there are times in everyone's life when we fail to pray and call out to God until we come to the end of our rope, and have no one left to turn to. Up until this moment in his life, where Samson found himself a prisoner, blinded and mocked, he did not employ prayer as he ought to have. He did not pray and ask of God whether to marry the Philistine, or whether he should go to Delilah, he did not enquire of God whether he should trust her or share his secret with her, but now, his eyes were finally opened even though they had been put out, and Samson cried out to God.

Samson was wise enough not to attempt to blame God for his predicament. He did not ask God why He had allowed him to come to this, or why God had not saved him from the hand of the Philistines. Samson was well aware he had done this to himself, by his rebellion, disobedience, and discounting of the calling to which he had been called.

Many a time, we get ourselves into situations solely of our own doing, then turn around and blame God for having allowed us to. It wasn't God's fault Samson was now without sight, bound and powerless. It was entirely Samson's doing. God counsels us, He shows us the way, but we must go in the way He shows us. If we set out on our own path, following our own heart, listening to the voice of another rather than God, then we cannot blame Him when we come to ruination.

'Strengthen me, this once,' was Samson's cry. When he had strength in abundance, he took it for granted, abused it, and used it unwisely, but now, seeing himself powerless, Samson cries out to God for the strength he once had.

Judges 16:30, "Then Samson said, 'let me die with the Philistines!' And he pushed with all his might, and the temple fell on the lords and all the people who were in it. So the dead that he killed at his death were more than he had killed in his life."

Thus ends the life of this man known as Samson, a man of contradictions, shortcomings and repeated failures. Perhaps in eternity we will be able to unravel the mystery of this man's life, and understand when forgiveness was granted him, since he is counted among the heroes of the faith long after his passing.

Some things are difficult to understand, and in those moments when human reason is not enough, we must trust in the wisdom of God, and realize He knows best. Samson prayed that he might die with the Philistines, and though it was a tragic and destructive prayer, though it was a prayer of vengeance, God answered it and restored his strength. Because his strength was restored, Samson was able to carry out what he'd purposed in his heart, and those he killed at his death were more than he had killed in his life.

May we learn from the life of Samson, and not wait as he did until the final moments to cry out to God. May we learn from the mistakes of others, and not repeat them ourselves, seeing the aftereffects of their disobedience and rebellion as object lessons and teachable moments.

THE PRAYER OF HANNAH

Hannah, the mother of the prophet Samuel, lived during the last days of the Judges of Israel. It was a very turbulent time for God's people, a season wherein everyone did what was right in their own eyes, making it up as they went along, and having no regard for the law of God or His commandments. Lawlessness reigned, and men were no longer concerned as to what the will of God was, or what the law of God said, but did as they saw fit, as benefited them, or pleased them in some way.

In other words, it was a lot like today except for all the technology and motorized vehicles. Men stray from God. It is a painful truth which we must acknowledge, and knowing it as truth, we must individually do our utmost not to be among those who stray. The way we do this is by continually keeping God's Word in our heart, and trusting the lamp that is the Scripture to illuminate the path before us, and prevent us from stumbling.

Men stumble when they begin to do what is right in their own eyes, rather than remain within the well-defined boundaries of Scripture. There has never been, nor will there ever be, an individual who, having walked in obedience to the Word and will of God, found themselves far from truth and off in the desert, away from the path of righteousness. It is rebellion in men's hearts that leads them to think they know better than God. Rebellious men assume that in doing what is right in their own eyes, they will still reach the same destination as the person who is following God the way He wants to be followed.

In Hannah's day, Eli's sons were doing what was right in their own eyes, and Israel paid the consequences.

The decline of a nation goes hand in hand with the decline of its spiritual leaders, and we see the sons of Eli, being corrupt and doing things that were unbecoming of priests. They did not know the Lord, yet they performed the tasks of the temple, out of habit, or due to it being an easy and rewarding career.

Tragically, much of the Old Testament, especially the negative aspects, mirror our day and age to an almost eerie degree. Today, as in the days of old we have our own version of the priests of the temple, whether we call them pastors, evangelists or preachers, and many of them, as was the case long ago, do it because they see it as a career rather than a calling.

Many of these men know not God nor do they know the power of God, yet they preach a version of spiritualized humanism which attracts many a soul because humanism requires neither righteousness nor holiness of the individual…just a cult of personality and a gift offering once in a while.

As those tasked with upholding the truth, the sons of Eli failed as miserably as many preachers and teachers are failing today. They did not teach truth, they did not preach the whole council of God, they were corrupt men just going through the motions, and because of this the whole of society became more debased, lawless, and vile. The spiritual condition of those who call themselves God's people, and the spiritual condition of the nation wherein they reside, are linked and interconnected. When those who ought to be the people of God abandon righteousness, holiness, and even morality, it is only a matter of time before those of the world begin to wax worse.

Judges 2:10-12, "When all that generation had been gathered to their fathers, another generation arose after them who did not know the Lord nor the work which He had done for Israel. Then the children of Israel did evil in the sight of the Lord, and served the Baals; and they forsook the Lord God of their fathers, who had brought them out of the land of Egypt and they followed other gods from among the gods of the people who were all around them; and they provoked the Lord to anger."

It was within this context that Hannah, the wife of Elkannah–by all accounts a godly man, who nevertheless had another wife by the name of Peninnah–comes before God with an ache in her heart, and a prayer of petition unmatched in passion and emotion.

The crux of Hannah's heartache being barrenness. In those days being barren was considered a curse for any married woman. Although Elkannah preferred Hannah over Peninnah, Peninnah tormented Hannah for years for not having any children, and not being able to bear sons.

There are many things we can glean from the prayer of Hannah, as well as the attitude and faithfulness of this amazing woman. Without doubt, Hannah is one of the noblest Hebrew women in the entire Bible. Even in her time of sadness and sorrow her faith and commitment to God are unwavering. She comes before God exhibiting not only faith, but an understanding of the divine in an age when her contemporaries had neither an understanding of God nor a desire to serve Him.

The people of Hannah's day, just as the priests of Hannah's day, were going through the motions, feigning worship, doing what they considered to be the bare minimum to still remain in God's good graces, all the while being corrupt and immoral in their conduct and lifestyle. It takes character to go against the tide, and to remain faithful when others around you are breaking faith. It takes character to intercede and plead with God from a position of hurt and pain, and still have the wherewithal to stand on His promises even when everything suggested the contrary.

Hannah was a woman who stood, and her prayer is a testament to faithfulness and obedience unto God.

Hannah is another in a long line of biblical figures we can relate to, because family issues are plentiful and frequent even among believers. Although we might not relate to Hannah in regards to the specificity of her issue, that her husband's other wife was making her life miserable, we can nevertheless understand heartache and sadness and sorrow.

No two problems are ever identical. There will always be a different nuance or a different context, but pain is pain, and everyone understands it. Hannah was a woman in anguish. Sorrow was her constant companion, and Peninnah would not let up, or miss an opportunity to remind her of her barrenness. Peninnah's provocations were not isolated to the homestead either. She continued mocking and attempting to make Hannah miserable even when they went to the house of the Lord. So vile and set upon malicious intent was this woman, that even being in the house of God did nothing to deter her from her singular task.

1 Samuel 1:7, "So it was, year by year, when she went up to the house of the Lord, that she provoked her; therefore she wept and did not eat."

We realize this was no back and forth banter, this wasn't needling someone in good humor; this was a vile and malicious woman attempting to squeeze the joy out of every moment of Hannah's life.

This goes to show how ugly a thing jealousy can be, and why as individuals we must guard our hearts against it. Peninnah was jealous that Elkanah preferred Hannah over her, and in her jealousy she lost sight of both reason and humanity. What was to be for Hannah a celebration of joy and of worship in the house of the Lord, turned into a season of sorrow and tears. Even her being in the house of the Lord is admirable, since many have a tendency to turn their backs on God when things aren't going their way, or when an expected entitlement never materializes in their lives.

Hannah was a woman who was barren, who suffered continually due to her husband's other wife. She was not even allowed to have some time alone with the Lord, because, even in His house Peninnah managed to open the wound afresh. Yet here, in God's house we find Hannah weeping and praying and crying out to God. Hannah did not abandon the house of the Lord when things didn't turn out as she'd hoped, she pressed in, and sought the face of the Lord all the more, knowing He was her only refuge and safe place.

Here she was, weeping and speaking in her heart with only her lips moving, and Eli, having watched her for a while concluded she was drunk.

1 Samuel 1:14, "So Eli said to her, 'How long will you be drunk? Put your wine away from you!'"

Few things in life are more hurtful than when we go to a spiritual authority for compassion and instead we find them judging and jumping to conclusions. Hannah was heartbroken, weeping, and praying silently, and Eli assumed she was drunk.

There is also a practical lesson we can glean from this entire exchange, one that will serve us well throughout life, that is, to never assume. If we are honest with ourselves, we will readily conclude we assume many things about many people throughout our lives. Even though we are taught from early youth not to judge a book by its cover, the first thing to make an impact—often times a permanent one—is an individual's appearance. If they are well kept, wearing a suit or an evening gown, we assume one thing. If they are a bit rough around the edges, or wearing a certain kind of garment, we assume something else. There have been instances in my life wherein a certain individual had a picture of me in their mind, and when their mental picture did not match the reality thereof, they grew disillusioned and distanced themselves.

We assume, and we expect, and we have a notion of what we think something ought to be like, and when it isn't, we don't admit we were wrong or that we judged harshly, but merely conclude that the individual wasn't wise enough to know better. It's inhumane to kick someone when they are down, and rather than assume the worst of an individual, it is wiser by far to take the time and listen to their sorrow, listen to their pain, and be a comfort if we can.

Even with the sorrow and humiliation Hannah was suffering, it is fascinating to see her spiritual state, and her character in the face of her trial and Eli's false accusation.

1 Samuel 1:15-16, "And Hannah answered and said, 'No, my lord, I am a woman of sorrowful spirit. I have drunk neither wine nor intoxicating drink, but have poured out my soul before the Lord. Do not consider your maidservant a wicked woman, for out of the abundance of my complaint and grief I have spoken until now.'"

Imagine for a second if this scenario had played out in a modern day church. A woman, weeping by the altar, moving her lips, praying silently to God, and the pastor or elder coming up to her and asking her how long she'd be drunk, and advising her to put her wine away from her. You and I know full well it would likely result in a lawsuit, citing defamation of character and other grievous things, and the pastor or elder would likely pay for their remark for the rest of their natural lives.

Instead of snapping at Eli, instead of starting to scream or make a scene, Hannah's answer was the epitome of spiritual maturity. 'No my lord, I am a woman of sorrowful spirit. I have drunk neither wine nor intoxicating drink, but have poured out my soul before the Lord.'

Hannah's soft spoken words did more to pierce the heart of Eli, than twice the screaming and stomping and acting out would have. Although this entire series is about prayer, from what it is, to learning from those who came before us and their prayer lives, when there are practical lessons we can learn and teachable moments we can grow from in the life of one of these biblical figures, I would be remiss if I didn't highlight it and mention it, if only in passing.

One of the most powerful lessons we can glean from the life of Hannah is that in our time of grief, of sadness, of desperation and hopelessness, we ought to run to God.

When trials descend, far too many believers have the tendency to withdraw themselves from among the children of God, to stop coming to the house of the Lord, and be on their own, by themselves, growing in their depression due to their isolation, and waxing worse. The house of the Lord and the people of God aren't there just for the good times. The household of faith isn't there just for the potlucks and birthday parties, it is a family, one body, which feels with the hurt and sadness of its members and helps in times of need and desperation. At least that's how it ought to be, and how Christ intended His church to be.

If you are hurting, if you are sorrowful, if trials abound in your life and you have no support or comfort from those you would call your brothers and sisters in Christ, then perhaps you should seek another church body, another fellowship which understands the true meaning of being one in Christ. It is dangerous and self-destructive to withdraw and isolate ourselves when hurt threatens to overwhelm us. Even though it is dangerous, it is nevertheless what many of us are predisposed to doing.

Both when my grandfather and my mother passed away, my reaction was to withdraw and isolate myself from everyone else and mourn alone. I continued in this manner until my wife came to me one day and said, 'you know everyone's feeling loss, and mourning just as much as you are. Perhaps it would be a good thing for everyone to be together during such a time.'

It was hard. I had to physically drag myself out of my apartment and go be with the rest of my family, almost against my will, but after a few hugs and a few tears, and a lengthy conversation I realized the wisdom of my wife's words. Hannah knew the house of the Lord was the place to be when everything was going wrong and when sorrow overflows. Though she wept, she wept before God, and prayed for resolution.

Pain and sorrow compel us to pray, and if they do not bring us to our knees, if they do not cause us to seek the face of God, nothing else will. Hannah understood the true meaning of prayer. She understood that true prayer was the pouring out of one's soul before the Lord, and these are the exact words she used when explaining to Eli what it was she had been doing.

When we pour our soul out to the Lord, we hold nothing back. We can't be selective as to what we pour out to the Lord when we pour our soul out to him. When we try to hold things back, we are as successful as trying to pour ice water into a glass without getting any of the ice cubes to spill over the edge. Tip the pitcher at enough of an angle, and everything will pour out, ice cubes and all.

Hannah had no one else to pour her heart out to but the Lord. Her husband didn't understand her pain, her husband's other wife was the source of her pain, and the priest thought she was drunk...but Hannah still had the Lord. No matter where you are, even though you might be far away from family and friends, even though you might be far removed from those you know, you can still go to the Lord, you can still pour out your soul to Him, and He will hear you.

All Hannah was doing was moving her lips. Her voice was not heard, for she was speaking in her heart, and still pouring her soul out to the Lord. Eli, having been a priest of the temple for many years, still found this behavior odd, so much so that he assumed Hannah was drunk, and this is why she could not speak the words she desired to speak.

Not everybody pours their soul out in the same manner. Some do so using words, some speak with the heart; some shed tears, others don't; some come before God with groaning, while others just fall on their face before Him. There is no wrong way to pour your soul out before the Lord!

No one on earth heard Hannah's cry, for it was a cry of the heart, but God in heaven did. The purpose of our prayers is not to be seen or heard by men. It is to be heard of God. So often we hear well-tailored prayers being prayed in churches, prayers from which the passion and emotion has been long removed, because they are prayers intended to impress, and not prayers intended to touch the heart of God. Be as Hannah in your prayers. Do not pray with the hope or expectation of being heard by anyone else, except for God. Do not pray to impress, do not pray to draw attention to how poetically you petition God, pour your soul out before the Lord, and He will hear and answer your pleas.

Hannah was unconcerned as to who might be watching her, or seeing her cry out to the Lord. She was unconcerned as to the image she was projecting, or what others might think of her. It was her and God, and all that mattered was that God was listening.

There are times when even those closest to us do not understand the pain and heartache we are going through. There are seasons in our lives when sadness crashes upon us like waves upon a rocky shore, and though we might try to explain it to family and friends, it is still something wholly personal. There is one who will always understand our heartache, our pain, our sadness, and our sense of loss, for He is the maker and creator of us all. He knows His creation better than the creation knows itself, and when we come before Him, not only does God listen to our prayers, He understands where we're coming from in regards to our emotional state at the present time.

When we view God as some emotionless taskmaster sitting in heaven just watching us bang our heads against the wall, we will undoubtedly be reticent in coming before Him and pouring our souls out to Him. When we view Him as the loving father that He is, when we see God as He is, the Creator whose love for mankind was such that He sent His only Son to die on our behalf, we will come before Him with open hearts, and pour out our sadness, our grief, our disappointment, our frustration, our anger, and our disillusionment.

Hannah's prayer was also a prayer of engagement...a promissory prayer of sorts. She prayed God would give her a male child, and in return she vowed Him the child would be consecrated into His service.

1 Samuel 1:11, "Then she made a vow and said, 'O Lord of hosts, if You will indeed look on the affliction of your maidservant and remember me, and not forget your maidservant, but will give your maidservant a male child, then I will give him to the Lord all the days of his life, and no razor shall come upon his head.'"

Hannah's vow was specific, and void of ambiguity. She did not quantify her promise with, 'if he can't get into medical school, then I will give him to the Lord all the days of his life,' she vowed outright that if the Lord gave her a male child, he would belong to the Lord. If you make a vow before God, and God answers your prayer, keep your vow. No one twisted your arm to make a vow to God, as no one twisted Hannah's arm to promise that if God gave her a male child she would dedicate Him to the service of the Lord.

Often times when we find ourselves in dire straits, we tend to come before God and make grandiose promises and vows. 'Lord, if you get me out of this predicament, I will do so and so for the rest of my life.' God, being faithful even when we are not, answers our prayers and gets us out of the predicament, but when it's our turn to keep our word, we either fail to do so completely, or find reasons and excuses to do what we promised only halfway.

It is far wiser not to make a vow in the first place, than having made a vow before God, go back on it, or pretend you never made it. God's record keeping is impeccable. Not one of us will stand before the throne of God on that day of days, and be able to convince Him that we didn't promise what we in fact promised, or that our promise was misinterpreted or misunderstood.

It's a dangerous thing trying to play lawyer with God, and attempt to find loopholes in the promises and vows you made to him. Trust me, God has read the fine print, He has read all the clauses, He has memorized the entire vow, and no excuse we bring before Him will suffice for the fact that we lied to His face, and that we are oath breakers.

Although this actually happened some years ago, let's presume there was a man who having just started a business made a vow to God that if he was successful in his venture, fifteen percent of what he brought in would go directly to ministries and outreaches. God heard the man's prayers, as well as his vow, and to everyone's surprise including his, his business took off, and significant amounts of money started to come in. Even if he had chosen to give fifteen percent off the top, this individual would still have had plenty for everything he needed to do, but the human heart being what he is, he started to go back on his vow.

At first, it was fifteen percent after taxes; a little while later it was fifteen percent after taxes and expenses, followed by taxes, expenses and salaries, and finally fifteen percent after taxes, expenses, and salaries, not to exceed $10,000 annually.

One thing led to another until this man's vow to God became the running joke in our small immigrant community because, to make matters worse, this individual had gotten up before the entire congregation and made his vow public.

Even with having broken his vow before God, the man's business went well for a couple years until it was discovered the bookkeeper he had hired had been embezzling and opening lines of credit on his company's behalf. Not only was he officially bankrupt, the man was also tied up in litigation over the credit lines for over a year.

When we fail to keep our vows before God, it is only a matter of time before He makes it painfully obvious that without Him we can do nothing. If you make a vow to God, follow through. Don't attempt to weasel out of it, and don't attempt to do less than what you promised you would do. Be a person of your word, and fulfill the promise you made to Him.

Ecclesiastes 5:4-5, "When you make a vow to God, do not delay to pay it; for He has no pleasure in fools. Pay what you have vowed. It is better not to vow than to vow and not pay."

Hannah made a vow, she kept it, and God honored her for it.

'Lord, give me a male child that I might give him to You." This was the essence of Hannah's prayer, and it was without doubt a beautiful desire. Why do we ask for what we ask? Why do we pray for what we pray? Is it to bring honor to God? Is it to further His kingdom? Or is it to fulfill our own selfish desires?

Hannah wanted a male child not so she might pamper him, or show him off, but so she might give Him to the Lord and in the service thereof. Her heart was pure as far as why she desired what she desired, and this is another reason God answered her prayer.

One of the things I find most disturbing in our modern church culture, is that we've taken greed and spiritualized it. We are told repeatedly, incessantly, and without respite that God wants us to be greedy, He wants us to want big houses and fancy cars and indoor, heated pools. Such messages play so well to the flesh, they connect so perfectly with our old nature that men who promulgate such aberrant doctrines are, in their own right, rich beyond their wildest imaginings.

Whether or not what we want brings glory to God has become a nonissue in today's church. We've taken care of that particular thorn in our side by redefining the will of God, and telling all who would hear that His will is no more than your happiness, ease, and comfort there on earth. 'God wants you to be happy!' How many times have you heard that fallacy spouted from behind a pulpit?

God wants you to be happy in Him! God wants you to make Him happy...to be pleasing unto Him.

Yet, when we speak of these things, men's immediate Pavlovian response is to bristle, and find some sort of reason why they think they ought to be happy, rich, and have everything they ever wanted in this present life. Praying has as much to do with the intent of our prayer, as it does with the actual act thereof. If our hearts are not right before God, though our lips might say one thing, He sees the inner heart, and knows why we are petitioning Him for a certain thing.

Hannah's heart was pure before God. Her desire was to return to the Lord that which He'd give her.

Another important lesson we can learn from Hannah's prayer, is that once God answered it, she returned before Him with prayers of thanks. Hannah returned to the place she has first prayed, the place where she poured her soul out to God, with the answer to her prayer in tow. She had given birth to a baby boy, named him Samuel, and had now come to give Him to the Lord as she had vowed.

1 Samuel 1:24-28, "Now when she had weaned him, she took him up with her, with three bulls, one ephah of flour, and a skin of wine, and brought him to the house of the Lord in Shiloh. And the child was young. Then they slaughtered a bull, and brought the child to Eli. And she said, 'O my lord! As your soul lives, my lord, I am the woman who stood by you here, praying to the Lord. For this child I prayed, and the Lord has granted me my petition which I asked of Him. Therefore I also have lent him to the Lord; as long as he lives he shall be lent to the Lord.' So they worshipped the Lord there."

For anyone who thinks it was easy for Hannah to do what she did, imagine the single most burning desire of your heart being fulfilled, then taking the fulfillment of that desire and giving it away. Hannah wanted nothing, more than she wanted a son. She had weaned him, cradled him, sung lullabies to him, and now she was giving him to the Lord. Since she had been barren, and Samuel was her only offspring, Hannah could have readily justified breaking her vow, at least to herself. From not having anyone to look after her in her old age, to not being able to see her child growing up, Hannah could have excused not bringing Samuel to the Lord as she had promised, but she chose to keep her vow.

Keeping one's vow is a choice!

God will not twist your arm into keeping your promises, nor is He a billing company sending you final notices for not paying your utilities bill. We either choose to be honorable servants keeping our vows and the promises we make, or dishonorable servants, who think we've put one over on God. Perhaps Hannah had left an impression, and Eli remembered her. There is also the chance that Eli had no clue as to whom this woman was, but after reminding him of the time he'd mistaken her for a drunk woman, and confirming that God had answered her prayers, they worshipped the Lord together.

It is a joyous thing when God answers our prayers. It is something for which we ought to be grateful, and thankful, and something of which we ought to tell others about as well. True servants of God will rejoice with us, and worship with us when we speak of the great and mighty things God has done. The bringing of Samuel to the house of the Lord was Hannah's public confession as to what God had done on her behalf and the prayer He had answered. Even if Eli remembered Hannah, he could not know what she had been praying for, for she did not espouse upon it at the time of their first encounter. Now, Hannah returned, to testify of the Lord's goodness, and confirm to one and all that God had not only heard her prayer, but answered it.

In reading Hannah's prayer as she came to deliver Samuel to the house of the Lord, we begin to understand the true depth of her relationship with God. Someone with a tangential knowledge of who God is could not have prayed such an eloquent and all-encompassing prayer. Hannah knew God and knew Him intimately.

For eleven verses, Hannah speaks of God's uniqueness, His omnipotence, His sovereignty, His mercy, His love, and His goodness. This was not a rehearsed prayer; it was not a prayer she memorized then came to deliver in the house of the Lord to impress Eli. It was a prayer of the heart birthed of the knowledge of the greatness of the God who can do all things, including make a barren womb fertile. When we come to possess knowledge of how great God is, we can't help but be in awe of Him. It is only when we do not know God, or when we possess only a superficial knowledge of His attributes that we can't find the words to give Him thanks.

Hannah was not a prophetess, yet she prayed a prophetic prayer. Hannah was not a scribe, or even the wife of a scribe, yet she knew God on a far deeper level than many of the elders and priests of her day. One need not attend seminary, be a minister, have a title, or possess a diploma in order to know God. God does not reveal

Himself to a select few who attend Bible College, but to all who desire to know Him, and fellowship with Him.

Our God is an equal opportunity God, who sees neither gender nor nationality, who sees neither age nor level of intelligence. If we seek Him, we will find Him, and if we desire a deeper walk with Him, He is but a prayer away. Even in her prayer of sorrow and grief, Hannah did not attempt to remake God in her image, or approach Him from a position of entitlement. 'If you will indeed look on the affliction of Your maidservant and remember me,' does not denote that Hannah was demanding God give her a son, or that she would be bitter if He didn't.

Hannah surrendered herself to the will of God for her life, knowing God knew best and trusting in His plan for her life. We could learn a lesson or two from this woman of the faith, and her humility and subservience to the authority of God are among the lessons we can learn.

Hannah knew the God to whom she prayed. She did not know about Him, she knew Him.

This is an important distinction many people today refuse to make, because their pride will not allow them to admit that though they know about God, they do not know God personally. I know about Tim Tebow...I don't know Tim Tebow. If I showed up at the man's house, he'd likely call the police and have me removed from his property, because although I know of him, I don't know him personally, and he doesn't know me. That, in a nutshell, is the difference between knowing about God, and knowing God Himself.

Most tragic by far, are those individuals who possessing knowledge about God, assume that they know Him. Such individuals are not few in number, but are in fact many, and in that day of which Jesus Himself speaks, they will have a rude if belated awakening.

Matthew 7:21-23, "Not everyone who says to Me, 'Lord, Lord,' shall enter the kingdom of heaven, but he who does the will of My Father in heaven. Many will say to Me in that day, 'Lord, Lord, have we not prophesied in Your name, cast out demons in

Your name, and done many wonders in Your name?' And then I will declare to them, 'I never knew you; depart from Me, you who practice lawlessness.'"

Taking the words of Jesus at face value, we come to understand that there are individuals who prophecy, cast out demons, and do many wonders in His name, without ever really knowing Him. They know of Him, they use His name as an authority, but as far as truly knowing Him, following after Him, and doing the will of the Father which is no less than to be holy, they are reticent. I submit that Hannah, simple, backward, and basic as some might consider her to be, knew the attributes of God and the power of God on a far deeper level than most seminary graduates today.

Chances are better than good that Hannah, this selfsame Hannah who knew God on such an intimate and intense level, was likely illiterate. She did not have her own leather-bound, red letter Bible with her name embossed on the cover, she did not have access to the vast ocean of theological treatise, doctrinal essays, books, recordings, videos, podcasts and blogs we do, yet she knew God far more profoundly than most do today.

Knowing God is about spending time with Him. Knowing God is about humbling ourselves and obeying rather than attempting to have a conversation by which we hope to somehow change His mind on a certain topic. Knowing God isn't just about knowing His love, it is also about knowing His justice, righteousness, holiness, and sovereignty.

When we know only one dimension of a multi-dimensional God, we know of Him, but don't really know Him. When we take one attribute of God and fashion our entire belief structure around that singular attribute, we are no longer worshipping the one true God in spirit and in truth, but a god of our own making, whom we've allowed to supplant the one true God in our hearts.

Philippians 3:10-11, "That I may know Him and the power of His resurrection, and the fellowship of His sufferings, being conformed to His death, if by any means, I may attain to the resurrection from the dead."

Now that we've already discussed Hannah's attitude while she prayed, I want to take some time and see what, if anything, we can glean from her actual prayer.

The first thing we notice when meditating upon Hannah's prayer is its specificity. Hannah was specific in her request to God. She wanted a male child, and it was a male child she asked God for. As she prayed she did not begin to address all the reasons why her prayer wouldn't, or couldn't be answered. She didn't say, 'if it doesn't happen I understand, I'm barren, and that's a big hurdle to jump over,' only that if God willed it, it would be thus.

There was faith in Hannah's prayer, not so much that what she was asking for would be given to her, but in God's ability to do what she was asking Him to do. She never, for an instant, doubted God's ability to make her fertile, or give her a male child. She did however understand that in order for her petition to be answered, it had to be in accordance with God's will.

Hannah prayed in faith, and God heard her prayer. Hannah likewise vowed to bring her son to the house of the Lord, and true to her word, she did as she promised. It is in the house of the Lord that Hannah's son remained, and she would come and bring him new clothes as he'd outgrow his old ones, but never once did she go before God and say, 'I've lent him to you long enough, now it's time for me to take him home.'

Hannah knew that her son being in the house of the Lord was the best possible place for him to be, even if it meant she would have to sacrifice in order for this to come to pass. This son, this answered prayer of Hannah's, grew up to be none other than Samuel the prophet of God, the man to whom God spoke audibly, and who became the spiritual leader of God's people during a very turbulent time in their history.

We have high hopes for our children. We want to see them get good educations, good jobs, good spouses, succeed in life, and make a future for themselves, but what we ought to hope and pray for more than anything else–especially given the times we are living in–is that they remain in the house of the Lord, and close to Him.

Daniel 11:32, "Those who do wickedly against the covenant he shall corrupt with flattery; but the people who know their God shall be strong, and carry out great exploits."

Do you want your son or daughter to succeed? Do you want your son or daughter to be strong and do great exploits? Then do your utmost to make certain they know their God. Bring them to the house of the Lord, commit them to Him, point them to the Christ, and stand in the gap on their behalf.

We live in a world full of distractions. We live in a world intent on building then reinforcing a wall between man and God, and if we are not watchful and vigilant, if we don't prioritize our lives in such a way wherein we make time to teach our children to walk in the way of the Lord, then the war's already lost and we might as well pack it all up and go about our business. We must see our children for the gifts and blessings of God that they are, and be single minded in our desire to see what He has entrusted us with, grow up to serve and obey Him.

Is it an easy task? No, it is not an easy task, and it is growing more difficult with each passing day. It is however a worthwhile task, one in which there is great joy and fulfillment, as well as great reward. Be specific in your prayers for your children, just as Hannah was specific in asking the Lord for a male child. Pray with specificity that their hearts will be tender toward Christ, that they will have abhorrence toward evil, that they will know and understand God, that they will feel His love, mercy, peace and joy, that they would walk in obedience.

There are times in life when it's fine to generalize…praying for our children is not one of those times.

Long before I was called to ministry, before I started preaching, writing, and teaching God's Word, my mother used to tell me stories of how my grandfather would pray for me while I was still a toddler. I was a sickly child (although you couldn't tell it by looking at me now), and though the doctors told my parents to prepare for the worst, my parents prayed for my healing until it came about. My mom used to say that while she and my father prayed for my general healing and wellbeing, my grandfather would pray that I would grow up big, and strong, and be a preacher of God's Word.

Although God answered my mother and father's prayers in that I received my healing, He also answered my grandfather's specific request in regards to me, wherein I grew up big, and strong, and have indeed become a preacher of God's Word.

Don't be afraid to be specific when you come before God. Don't be reticent in pouring your soul out to Him, and telling Him the desire of your heart. Trust and believe that He is able. Stand on His promises, and with sincerity petition Him for that with which you desire to further His kingdom and magnify His name.

Hannah's journey began with a prayer made in faith. It continued with a vow to return unto God that which God would give, and due to her faith and faithfulness we have the shining example of what it means to be a man of God, in her son Samuel.

THE PRAYER OF SAMUEL

Since Samuel was a man of lifelong prayer, it is near impossible to choose one prayer out of the many the Word of God tells us Samuel prayed. As such, we will be discussing the broader context of Samuel's prayer life, and include more than one of his prayers in our study.

Samuel was promised to God from before his conception. His mother Hannah pleaded with the Lord, and promised if He would grant her a male child, she would consecrate him unto the Lord, and bring him to the house of the Lord. Hannah kept her word, and once he had been weaned, Samuel was brought to the tabernacle of the Lord. From early youth Samuel learned the ways of God ministering before the Lord even as a child.

It was in his youth that God began to speak to Samuel, and one of his first assignments, was to tell his mentor, Eli, the man who had cared and watched over him since the day he had been brought to the tabernacle, that God had judged his family because he had failed to reign in his two sons.

As far as historical context goes, Samuel was also the last judge of Israel. Even though he was the last judge in Israel, he was also the greatest judge Israel had ever known, simultaneously serving as a priest in the tabernacle of the Lord and as a prophet of God.

Although Samuel was a man of multiple callings, and was even assigned to oversee the transition of Israel to a unified nation with a single king, he always made time for prayer. We find him in the presence of God, praying to Him, petitioning Him, and be-seeching Him as often as any Old Testament figure barring a couple exceptions. Perhaps his mother had told him the story of how she had been barren, had prayed, and had been blessed with a son as an answer to her prayers. Perhaps he saw his mentor Eli praying, and coming before the altar of the Lord with regularity. Whatever sparked Samuel's awareness of how important prayer was, it stayed with him all of his days, and he continued living a life of prayer and supplication throughout his journey here on earth.

The first thing we can learn from Samuel, even before we begin to discuss the prayers he prayed, is the importance of knowing how important prayer is in the life of a believer. Samuel knew prayer was paramount in his life, and though for many of us the sheer volume of his responsibilities might seem impossible to manage, he always made time to come before the Lord and have fellowship with Him.

We always make time for what we deem as necessary in our lives. We always make time for those things we think we can't do without. Admittedly, some things such as eating periodically, drinking water, and sleeping are indispensable and necessary, but other things we do on a daily basis are anything but. We squander the most precious resource we've been given i.e., time, chasing after childish distractions, all the while talking ourselves into believing we can't live without them.

If you were to make a list of the indispensable things in your life, would prayer be near the top of that list? If not, why not?

Samuel understood from an early age how indispensable, necessary, and paramount prayer was in the life of one who desires to hear the voice of God, have a relationship with God, and know the heart of God. Even though his responsibilities grew as he grew, the foundation of Samuel's prayer life had already been firmly established, and whatever else he was called to do, from anointing the first king of Israel, to anointing his replacement, Samuel still found time to pray. If a man tasked with anointing kings, prophesying over nations and serving as priest in the tabernacle of the Lord found time to pray, you and I have no excuse.

Whether we have to clean the house, do laundry, take the kids to soccer practice, mow the lawn, not to mention surf the net, watch television, or a hundred other things that occupy our time some of which are utterly pointless, chances are we still won't be as busy as Samuel. If Samuel found time to pray, then we ought to be able to find time to pray.

It all boils down to one solitary question: 'do I think prayer an important enough component in my spiritual walk to sacrifice other less important things in order to make time to pray?'

It is not a question I can answer for you, nor can you answer it for me. We are each responsible for what we do with the time we've been given, how we use it, and what we apply ourselves to. If we apply ourselves to building our relationship with God and discovering more of Him, then prayer will be a priority in our lives, and we will do away with the vain, foolish, or unproductive things in our daily activities in order to make time for it.

If, however, God and the knowledge of Him are at the bottom of the list, somewhere between getting a new air freshener for the car and picking up the latest spiritualized humanism drivel being promoted by the currently popular television preacher, then we will always find something else to do in lieu of going to our prayer closet, and spending some time with God. Men of God are not born men of God. Men of God are called, then molded, chiseled, built up, equipped, finding their fulfillment in God, and the presence of Him alone. The lights, the cameras, the pulpits, the book signings, the interviews, are all distractions which take away from a man of God's primary purpose…to spend time with his Master, fellowship with Him, and grow in the knowledge of Him.

God speaks to us through His Word, and we in turn speak to Him through prayer. Just the knowledge that we can come before the Creator of all that is, both seen and unseen, ought to compel us and inspire us to spend more time in prayer than we do. What could be more fulfilling in this life than knowing you can speak to God, and that He is listening? You could meet the president of every nation, shake their hand, and have tea, and it still wouldn't compare with being able to speak to God, and having Him speak back.

We've grown so accustomed to certain things that we have stripped all the wonder and majesty from them. Prayer is one of the things we've allowed to become a usual thing in our lives, so much so that we often forget what it is we are doing when we pray. When I pray, I, Michael Boldea, the son of a glassblower and the grandson of a potato farmer, am speaking to God almighty, Creator of heaven and earth, giver of life and existence as we know it.

Who am I to have such an honor? Who am I to have the privilege of communicating and fellowshipping with the God of the universe? And yet, so often, we say a few hurried words on our way out the door, or before biting into our meal, as though we were doing Him the favor by uttering a prayer.

There is one other undeniable trait in Samuel–as well as all the men of God whom God used as vessels of honor–his reverence for the person of God. Every biblical figure who was a man or woman of prayer was also deeply reverential toward God. They knew God, and because they knew God they had reverence and veneration for Him. Lack of reverence for the house of God, the things of God, and the person of God is one of my personal pet peeves, and whenever I see it in individuals who ought to know better, I just can't abide it.

Only one who does not understand who God is or know the person of God both intimately and through the prism of Scripture, can be so indifferent as to be irreverent when coming before Him. Not only is irreverence practiced in many a church, it is encouraged by certain leaders who insist God is nothing more than our buddy, our pal, our "go to" individual in case of emergency, but nothing so imposing as King, Creator, Master or Lord.

Samuel the prophet of the Lord is counted among the many notables who understood the nature of God and as a direct result came before Him with reverence and humility. Even the people realized Samuel was a man of prayer, and that His prayers were received of God.

1 Samuel 7:8, "So the children of Israel said to Samuel, 'do not cease to cry out to the Lord our God for us, that He may save us from the hand of the Philistines.'"

The people knew Samuel was interceding on their behalf. They knew Samuel was crying out to the Lord for them, and they asked him not to cease doing this, so God might save them from the hand of the Philistines.

It's good to know someone is praying for us. I have individuals who will write me from time to time and say, 'you're in our prayers, keep doing what you're doing.' Knowing that I'm in their prayers, knowing that someone is crying out to the Lord on my behalf, gives me strength and a new desire to keep pressing on, and doing the work to which I have been called to the best of my ability. The knowledge that you are in someone's prayers is a source of strength. The people knew Samuel's prayers mattered, they knew God heard when he petitioned and cried out on their behalf, and they asked him not to stop.

Although Samuel loved the people of Israel to the point that by their own admission he 'cried out to the Lord on their behalf,' he did not compromise the truth, or attempt to sidestep sensitive issues in regards to their obedience toward God. You can love the people of God, and still speak the truth with boldness. You can love the people of God and still call sin by its name, and call the household of faith to repentance.

In recent years we've been conditioned to believe that if someone challenges our lifestyle, if they point out inconsistencies or outright sin in our lives and counsel us to repent, they are unloving, judgmental, unkind, and not possessing the heart of Christ.

Nothing could be further from the truth!

Someone who will take the time to challenge you because the Bible compels them to is not hateful, intolerant, or bigoted, but rather loving, kind and obedient toward God. In spite of the fact that he was raised in the tabernacle, and did not grow up in a family of warriors or soldiers, Samuel was a bold man who did not shy away from doing his duty, and saying the difficult thing when the difficult thing was required. Samuel's boldness and courage extended to the point of calling the king of Israel a fool for not keeping the commandment of the Lord.

In our day and age it seems we associate men of God with soft spoken, non-confrontational, perpetually smiling individuals who only have kind and positive words to say to us, even though our lives and conduct are not in accordance with Scripture. It was not always so, and as recently as twenty years ago, there were still men of God who walked in His authority, and spoke the truth fearlessly to anyone regardless of the position they held or the power they wielded. Unfortunately, now when we need men of boldness and action more than ever before, such men grow rarer by the day.

Samuel did not pray because it was his job to pray for others, nor did he pray because of who might be listening in on his prayers. Samuel did not pray out of habit or routine, he prayed because he understood that to not pray for the people was to sin against the Lord.

1 Samuel 12:23, "Moreover, as for me, far be it from me that I should sin against the Lord in ceasing to pray for you; but I will teach you the good and the right way."

Samuel considered it sin to cease praying for the people of Israel. He considered it sin to cease coming before the Lord and seeking His face, even though the people had chosen contrary to Samuel's wishes. Even so, Samuel vowed that he would continue to teach them the good and right way. A teacher's duty is to teach; a pupil's duty is to receive the teaching. I must do my utmost to make certain that at the end of the day, and at the end of my life, there is no blood on my hands, and that I've preached the whole counsel of God.

The duty of those who hear me speak, or read what I write, is to receive the teaching, and allow it to take root in their heart, or reject it outright. My duty is to preach the truth; your duty is to receive the truth.

Samuel knew his prayers would only go so far. He knew that whether Israel thrived or was judged depended on the people and whether or not they feared the Lord and served Him in truth with all their heart.

1 Samuel 12:24-25, "Only fear the Lord, and serve Him in truth with all your heart; for consider what great things He has done for you. But if you still do wickedly, you shall be swept away, both you and your king."

We can pray for a nation, cry out for a nation, intercede for a nation, but as long as the nation does not fear the Lord and serve Him with all its heart, God will still judge and the nation will still be swept away. Whether speaking of America, Romania, or any other nation where the children of God happen to reside, though God may hear our prayers for a nation, if the nation rebels against Him, does wickedly, and refuses to repent, He will judge it even with believers having prayed for the nation in question.

Does this mean we ought to stop interceding for the nations we pray for? No, for ceasing to pray for a nation would be as sinning against the Lord. What I am saying is, if God chooses to judge a nation even after we've prayed and interceded for it, may we be wise enough to understand that God did not disregard our prayers, or refuse to hear them, but that His justice demanded wickedness be judged.

Another area in which Samuel excelled was the knowledge of God's expectations of His people. Samuel knew that omission was still a sin, and this is the reason he was so adamant in not ceasing to pray for the people.

Often times professing Christians are seen by non-Christians in either a place they ought not to be, doing something they ought not to be doing, wearing something they ought not to be wearing, or saying something they ought not to be saying, and even non-believers shake their head and say, 'he ought to know better than that!' We have no excuse for not knowing better because we have the Word of God, and it teaches us what we must do, how we must live, and what we must repent of.

Samuel knew better than to not pray for God's people, and knowing better meant that if he chose to cease praying for them, it would be counted as sin. We all know God rejoices when He sees His children desire fellowship with Him. We know our prayers are as sweet smelling incense or sacrifice to God, so we have no excuse for circumventing prayer, or thinking it unnecessary in our modern age. We read or hear of God speaking to regular, ordinary, everyday men and women, and feel a twinge of jealousy because it isn't us. We read the Scriptures and see the mighty ways in which God used certain individuals, and can't help but think to ourselves, 'I wish I could have been there to see that...I wish I could have lived in those times.'

What we often gloss over, or choose to ignore, are the endless hours such individuals spent in prayer and supplication before God, how they nurtured and cemented their relationship with the

Lord for years, even decades, until He started speaking to them and using them in such magnificent ways. We all want to be used of God, but none of us want to put in the time required to get to that spiritual place of being ready to be used of God.

There was a time when even Samuel did not know the voice of the Lord. There was a time when even Samuel did not know the Lord well enough to approach Him, but through obedience, humility, and a desire to be pleasing to the Lord, he became the man we know today as the last, and greatest judge of God's people, one of the most renowned prophets of the Old Testament, and the man for whom two books of the Bible are named. To see him as he was, freshly weaned from his mother and brought to the house of the Lord, no one could have guessed at the man Samuel would become, and the ways in which God would use him.

Before he could be used of God however, he had to grow in the knowledge of God, and we grow in the knowledge of God by diligently studying His Word, and spending time in prayer.

The first of Samuel's prayers we will discuss is a short yet profound prayer he prayed on behalf of Israel. Israel was in a deplorable state once more. They had strayed from the one true God, given their hearts over to idols, and even sinned with the Ark of the Lord. For twenty years they had forgotten about the Ark of the Lord, they had dismissed all the warnings of God, but finally, as they saw the Philistines subjugate them to the point of slavery, they turned their hearts toward God once more and began to seek Him.

As is often the case, when we refuse to heed the loving warnings of a loving God, He removes His hand of protection and gives free reign to our enemies. Oftentimes we tend to believe that God Himself must judge, and punish, but all that is required for a nation to be upended is for God to remove His protection from around it. The nation's enemies will do the rest.

God had long since removed His protection from around Israel, for they had not heeded His words, and now when they saw that without Him they were powerless, impotent, and at the mercy of the Philistines, they began to cry out to God, and turn their hearts back to Him again. When the desire for God is sparked in men's hearts, when they begin to lament after the Lord, a man whom God has been preparing to lead His people will always make an appearance, and compel them to repentance and righteousness.

1 Samuel 7:3, "Then Samuel spoke to all the house of Israel, saying, 'if you return to the Lord with all your hearts, then put away the foreign gods and the Ashtoreths from among you, and prepare your hearts for the Lord, and serve Him only; and He will deliver you from the hand of the Philistines.'"

Notice, Samuel didn't come before the people and say, 'it is well that you lament after the Lord, now I will pray for you and everything's going to be alright.' Samuel knew that without the people's hearts turning fully toward the Lord and abandoning their idols altogether, his prayer would not have amounted to much. The people desired to follow after God, and Samuel told them what they needed to do in order to make this happen. Samuel was direct when it came to telling the people what God required of them. If they really did desire to return to the Lord, then they needed to put away the foreign gods from among them, and prepare their hearts for the Lord, serving Him only.

The people lamented after the Lord, but as yet they had not put away their idols and false gods. In their hearts they desired the one true God, but as yet had taken no practical steps toward reconciliation with Him. We know God remains the same from age to age and generation to generation, yet somehow we've allowed ourselves to be deceived into believing He no longer requires the same turning away from the sins in our lives, and the wholehearted embracing of Him. God's requirements of those who desire to come to Him have remained the same. Somewhere along the way however, men deemed putting away their idols and preparing their hearts for the Lord too difficult a task.

Samuel knew he could not do on behalf of the people what was incumbent upon them to do themselves. He could neither give up their idols for them, nor turn their hearts to the Lord. All Samuel could do was show them the path, and give them the instruction. Whether or not they followed and obeyed was entirely up to them.

This theme runs through the entire Bible. Solomon, for example, a couple of generations after Samuel, clearly understood the relationship between having a wholehearted devotion to God and having your prayers heeded by God.

> *1 Kings 8:48-49, "And when they return to You with all their heart and with all their soul in the land of their enemies who led them away captive, and pray to You toward their land which You gave their fathers, the city which You have chosen and the temple which I have built for Your name: then hear in heaven Your dwelling place their prayer and their supplication and maintain their cause."*

The preceding is an excerpt from a much longer prayer prayed by Solomon for the people of Israel. Being wise as he was, Solomon knew that unless the people returned to the Lord with all their heart and all their soul, God would not hear their prayer and supplication, nor maintain their cause.

Whenever discussing Israel of old, we tend to forget that they were the people of God. The Jews were, as they continue to be, God's people, but even they would not have the ear of God unless their hearts were right before Him. Just because we raised a hand in church does not mean we get to cut to the front of the line, or discount God's pre-established parameters in regards to what He demands of those calling themselves His children. If Israel didn't get a pass, if Israel had to repent, turn their hearts toward God and seek His face in order to be heard of God, then we likewise must break ties with those things keeping us tethered to this world, and surrender our all to Him.

Israel had seen the light. They had realized the impossibility of victory without the aid of God, and it is within this context that Samuel asked for all of Israel to be gathered at Mizpah, that he might pray for them.

> *1 Samuel 7:5-6, "And Samuel said, 'Gather all Israel to Mizpah, and I will pray to the Lord for you.' So they gathered together at Mizpah, drew water, and poured it out before the Lord. And they fasted that day, and said there, 'we have sinned against the Lord.' And Samuel judged the children of Israel at Mizpah."*

It was here that the people acknowledged their sin. It was here that the people acknowledged their need to be forgiven and reconciled unto God, having been made ready to make the necessary changes in order to facilitate this outcome.

'Clean house before you invite God in.' This was the essence of Samuel's message to the people. God is not willing to share space with another, nor is He willing to have only half your heart. With God it's either all or nothing at all.

It is because we've allowed for half measures when it comes to serving God that we now have an entire generation of lukewarm, passionless individuals roaming about calling themselves Christians, believers, and sons and daughters of God. There can be no half measures when it comes to following after God. Either we belong to Him, or we belong to the world. Either we serve Him, or we serve another. Samuel understood this, and because he understood it, he was able to relay it to the people.

Romans 8:13-14, "For if you live according to the flesh you will die; but if by the Spirit you put to death the deeds of the body, you will live. For as many as are led by the Spirit of God, these are the sons of God."

When it comes to spiritual things, we don't like seeing the word 'if' anywhere, either in the vicinity or in close proximity. As put off as we might by this two letter word however, we cannot deny its existence, nor deny its inclusion within the pages of Scripture. The Word of God uses the word 'if' often, in order to denote conditionality. If we prepare our hearts, if we put iniquity far from us, if we remove it from our tents, then we could be steadfast and not fear, and lift up our face without spot.

Only after telling the people of their need to repent and put away their gods and idols, only after telling them they needed to turn their hearts wholly toward God, did Samuel pray, and intercede on behalf of Israel.

1 Samuel 7:9, "And Samuel took a suckling lamb and offered it as a whole burnt offering to the Lord. Then Samuel cried out to the Lord for Israel, and the Lord answered him."

Samuel could have cried out to the Lord for Israel before Israel turned their hearts back to the Lord, but the Lord would not have answered his prayers. Knowing this, Samuel laid the groundwork to ensure that when he did cry out to the Lord, the Lord would not only hear him, but answer him.

Another moment in the prayer life of Samuel worthy of meditation and contemplation took place when he, having grown older in years, was disrespected by the elders of Israel. In the elders' defense, Samuel's sons had not followed in their father's footsteps, and they had turned aside after dishonest gain, took bribes, and perverted justice. Since Samuel was getting on in years, it was his sons who would have been the new judges of the people, and the people realized how far removed in character Samuel's sons were from Samuel himself.

> *1 Samuel 7:4-6, "Then all the elders of Israel gathered together and came to Samuel at Ramah, and said to him, 'Look, you are old, and your sons do not walk in your ways. Now make for us a king to judge us like all the nations.' But the thing displeased Samuel when they said, 'Give us a king to judge us.' So Samuel prayed to the Lord."*

No longer did the people want a judge to rule over them, they wanted a king to judge them, like all the nations surrounding them already had. Bringing up Samuel's age was just an excuse, a way for these elders to make their point without really stating why they no longer desired his guidance and counsel. Samuel knew he was getting old, no one needed to point it out, but he was still strong enough wherein he could perform the tasks God had given him without complaint.

What the elders really wanted was a change. They wanted to be like the rest of the nations. They wanted a king, and even if Samuel would have been in the prime of his life, they still would have found a reason or excuse to remove him and bring in a king.

What I love about Samuel's reaction to hearing the elders speak to him the way they did, is that instead of screaming at them, beating his chest and asking them if they knew who they were talking to, asking them to leave, or doing a myriad of other things, Samuel prayed to the Lord. We see the character of Samuel in this often overlooked action, because he did not attempt to defend himself, he did not attempt to rise to their provocations, he went and prayed to the Lord.

It is in times of hardship, stress, opposition or turmoil that our true character is revealed. When everything is going well, it is easy to feign piety, it is easy to feign a tender heart and a humble spirit, but when everything in our lives is upended, when what was once sweet is now sour, our true character is revealed in how we deal with such situations, and how we react toward them.

Samuel went to God in prayer, because he knew no one could clarify the situation better than the One who had spoken to him since early youth, the One who guided him, instructed Him, empowered him, and comforted him. Is God the first one we run to when things are going south? Is He the first one we talk to when the unexpected happens, and we are left stunned and speechless?

Samuel knew there was no one else he could turn to in such a time. He prayed to God because he knew God has all the answers. It's never hit or miss with God. We never find He is out of town, on vacation, or too busy to speak to us, nor that He has grown so successful in His chosen field that He no longer gives us the time of day. God hears our prayers, and answers our prayers. He desires to fellowship with His creation, and be in communion with us.

We're not imposing when we approach God. We come before Him boldly, knowing He will receive us and hear us. Any excuse we might have for not coming before God in prayer, for not pouring out our souls whenever the need arises, is unfounded and has no basis in fact. God knows the need for man to communicate with Him is a fundamental one. Man is fragmented and incomplete until he establishes a relationship with God the Father, and learns to dialogue, fellowship and communicate with Him.

Even the Christ went to prayer in His moments of hardship and trial. Even the Christ prayed to the Father as His time drew near. We see these great men of the faith, and even Christ Jesus Himself spending time in prayer and supplication before the Father, and somehow we still convince ourselves we are above the need to pray and fellowship with God. They might have needed to spend time in prayer, but they didn't know the secrets of being self-assured, and self-confident.'

The heroes of the Bible spent time in prayer because they realized only God could provide a remedy for their heartache, their pain, and their disappointment. Samuel got attacked by the elders of Israel on all fronts. His competence was called into question, his family was maligned, and his labors in leading Israel were marginalized, because the people wanted something new, something different, something like the rest of the nations had.

New isn't always better, and this is also true of churches and fellowships who are so focused on being relevant and engaging of our modern culture, that they abandon the truth of Christ and the gospel for the sake of relevance.

Another glimpse into the heart of Samuel, and the true measure of love and faithfulness this man possessed, is when God rejects Saul as king, and tells Samuel as much. Keep in mind, the elders swept Samuel to the side in order to have a king, and now the king which had been anointed to rule and judge over Israel, was being rejected of God. For most people this would have been the perfect time to gloat. It would have been the perfect time to point out how the elders had gotten it wrong, and demand an apology. Instead of doing what most men would have done, Samuel proceeds to do what Christ would later teach us we must do, and that is pray for Saul and be grieved by God's rejection of him.

> *1 Samuel 15:10-11, "Now the word of the Lord came to Samuel, saying, 'I greatly regret that I have set up Saul as king, for he has turned back from following Me, and has not performed My commandments.' And it grieved Samuel, and he cried out to the Lord all night."*

Even though Saul had essentially replaced him as far as judging over the people was concerned, Samuel still found it in his heart to cry out to the Lord all night, being grieved by God's rejection of Saul as king. It is within certain contexts, and certain moments that we discover men's true hearts. It is in those instances wherein they do not know they are being watched, wherein they are not trying to impress, or project an image that the true character of an individual rises to the surface.

The Word of the Lord had come to Samuel informing him of Saul's failures, and it grieved him to the point of crying out to the Lord all night. He didn't go into the square, he didn't gather the people, he didn't schedule an extra special night of prayer and intercession for the king, he cried out to the Lord where he was, without drawing attention to himself. Samuel didn't pretend to be grieved, he was grieved. Even though the removal of Saul would both justify and solidify his own position, Samuel cried out to the Lord on behalf of Saul.

Uncommon practices draw the eye, and Samuel being grieved for the sake of Saul drew my eye. You don't often find those who feel as though they have been cast aside praying for the individual who replaced them. You don't often find an individual being grieved and crying out to the Lord all night on behalf of another, who succeeded him, and appropriated his authority. Samuel's true heart and character shone bright in his actions, and we see both the faithfulness and tenderness of this prophet of God in his prayer for Saul, the king whom God rejected.

1 Samuel 16:1, "Then the Lord said to Samuel, 'how long will you mourn for Saul, seeing I have rejected him from reigning over Israel? Fill your horn with oil, and go; I am sending you to Jesse the Bethlehemite. For I have provided Myself a king among his sons.'"

Even though Samuel 'went no more to see Saul until the day of his death,' he continued to mourn for Saul. This went on for so long, that the Lord Himself said to Samuel, 'how long will you mourn for Saul?' Just because someone chooses the path of rebellion, it does not mean we ought to stop praying, interceding, and even mourning for them. Just because someone chooses to turn their back on the truth, it does not mean we ought not to remember them in our petitions to the Lord. As long as they have breath they can still repent and turn toward God.

Yes, Samuel separated himself from Saul and no longer went to see him, but he continued to pray for him in earnest.

1 Samuel 23:2, "Therefore David inquired of the Lord, saying, 'Shall I go and attack these Philistines?' And the Lord said to David, 'Go and attack the Philistines and save Keilah.'"

THE PRAYER OF DAVID

The history of David is a complex one. Depending on whom you ask, opinions about David are wide-ranging and varied. For some, David will always be the boy with the slingshot who took down the giant. For others, David will always be the king of Israel, the man who replaced Saul and fathered Solomon. For others still, David will always be the man who gave in to his temptations, and orchestrated a plot to take Bathsheba from her husband.

David was all these things and more. He was also a man of prayer, and one whom God considered to be after His own heart.

By all accounts David was an imperfect man. There is no disputing the facts as they are plainly laid out in Scripture, and often times David's behavior is cringe worthy. Even so, his ability to repent endeared him toward God, because when David repented it was not just lip service or an attempt to appease a wrathful God, but true and heartfelt repentance which brought about change in him.

What do we know about David and his prayer life?

There is more written about David in the Scriptures than almost any other individual. He is a central figure within the pages of the Bible, arguably the greatest warrior-king Israel has ever known, and the writer of many of the psalms we have in the book of Psalms.

Looking back on David's life, none would have guessed that the boy assigned to watch over his father's sheep would end up being king over all of Israel. No one could doubt the hand of God at work as a shepherd boy was anointed to rule over Israel, especially one who happened to be the youngest of eight siblings, coming from a family of little to no renown.

Only a fool despises small beginnings, and where we end up in life has very little to do with the benefits we were afforded in our adolescence and everything to do with God's plan and purpose for our life. Advantages in life do not guarantee success, nor do disadvantages in life guarantee failure.

It was from a fragile age that David developed a reverence for God. Since he spent his days and nights alone in the fields watching over his father's sheep, David's awe of God grew in him organically and independently. Unlike Samuel, David was not raised in the temple or the tabernacle. His relationship with God grew out of an individual desire to know Him, and a continual meditation upon the person of God and the things of God.

Because the foundation of his relationship with God had already been established, when David is sent to the battlefront with supplies for his older brothers and hears Goliath mocking God, he accepts the challenge of fighting the giant and fells him with a single stone.

We can see by David's reaction to Goliath's mocking, that his relationship with God was personal and intimate. He was deeply affected by the mockery and disdain brought to the name of his God, and David knew God would stand with him if he stood to defend the name of God.

In retrospect, David being thrust upon the national stage of Israel seems to have been either accidental or fortuitous in the eyes of the world, but providential to those who believe in the sovereignty of God. To those of the world, even if they believe in the historical David, and that he felled the giant Goliath, they are reticent when it comes to accepting that the hand of God was guiding this young shepherd every step of the way.

To those who believe, however, the hand of God on David's life from early youth is undeniable, and we see God not only guiding him, but protecting him and working through him. One stone, one slingshot, and a boatload of courage, made David a household name overnight.

David did not go seeking fame; he didn't go to the battlefront hoping to encounter some Philistines, never mind the biggest Philistine of them all, he was there because his father had sent him with food for his brothers, and his willingness to believe God beyond what he could see in the physical facilitated his encounter with Goliath.

Often times, we never confront our Goliath because we think ourselves too weak to vanquish him.

David was well aware that in and of himself there was little to no chance of defeating a man Goliath's size. Seeing as even the king and all his warriors feared confronting this Philistine, for David to think that he could do it was either madness, or faithfulness toward God. Yes, sometimes our faithfulness might seem like madness to some, but our only concern ought to be what God thinks of us, and not what men might think of us.

I've known men whom God told to leave thriving businesses and move halfway around the world to work in some of the poorest regions on the planet, just offering aid, comfort and shelter. To human reason, this seems as foolish as taking a slingshot and a few stones and going to confront a giant in full armor who had likely spent most of his adult life taking lives. It is in obedience that we see the power of God made manifest in our lives. We can talk about obedience, talk about others who are being obedient, but until we step out in faith, and walk in obedience we will not see the manifest power of God.

These men I mentioned, who left everything they knew to go and be a comfort to others, see the power of God manifest in their lives by way of provision, as well as supernatural healings and miracles. They are seeing these victories, just as David saw his victory, because they are following through, and walking in the obedience God demands of His children.

Since this is not a teaching on the boldness or obedience of David, but rather about his prayer life, as much as it pains me to leave treasure unearthed–since the man's entire life is a goldmine of teachable moments–we will shift our focus to his prayers, and his prayer life.

Whether he found himself in the valley or on the mountaintop David was consistently a man of prayer. David prayed when times were good and when times were bad, when victory was his, and when he suffered defeat. David was not a man to pray only when he needed God's help. He genuinely loved being in the presence of the Lord, communing with Him, and being in fellowship with Him. As such, we see David spending time in prayer both when he is a sheepherder as well as when he is king, when he is preparing to go up against Goliath, as well as when he's basking in the victory of having vanquished him.

In the most difficult of times, we find David running to God, and strengthening himself in Him. We see a man who knew his limitations in David, and who realized human strength, intelligence, and aptitude will only carry you so far. Any further, and you have to trust God. We see David's willingness to humble himself before the Lord in every difficult circumstance of his life. We see his character, even though he was not a perfect man, and we see His dependency upon the Lord.

One of the most telling events of David's life was also one of the most heartbreaking. It was during his campaign against the Amalekites, shortly after they had burned Ziklag with fire and taken captive the women and those who were there. It was a dark time for David, his own wives having been taken captive, and his men growing angrier with each passing minute because of what had occurred.

1 Samuel 30:6, "Then David was greatly distressed, for the people spoke of stoning him, because the soul of all the people was grieved, every man for his sons and his daughters. But David strengthened himself in the Lord."

His wives taken captive, his men ready to stone him, and rather than attempt anything of his own volition, David strengthened himself in the Lord. When we come to know the Lord, we realize we have strength in Him.

What does a prayer of a man dependent upon God sound like? What attributes are found within the prayers themselves that differentiate them from other prayers?

We have to go back a few pages in David's story to find the first prayer assigned to David within the pages of Scripture is one wherein he inquires of the Lord whether he should go to war.

The Philistines had gone to war against a place called Keilah, and upon being informed of this, rather than make a spur of the moment decision as to whether he ought to attack the Philistines, or stay out of the skirmish, David inquired of the Lord.

1 Samuel 23:2, "Therefore David inquired of the Lord, saying, 'Shall I go and attack these Philistines?' And the Lord said to David, 'Go and attack the Philistines and save Keilah.'"

David asked, and God answered. It should have been as simple as that, but when David informed his men they were about to attack the Philistines, his men reminded him of their perilous predicament, and how they were already fearful, without having to engage the enemy.

1 Samuel 23:3-4, "And David's men said to him, 'Look, we are afraid here in Judah. How much more then if we go to Keilah against the armies of the Philistines?' Then David inquired of the Lord once again. And the Lord answered him and said, 'Arise, go down to Keilah. For I will deliver the Philistines in your hand.'"

God did not rebuke David for inquiring of Him again. Even though God had already told him to go and attack the Philistines, David's men had begun to filter what God had said through the prism of human reason, and had concluded that they were fearful on their own turf, without having to confront an enemy. Because of their fear, David inquired of the Lord once more, and the Lord reconfirmed the victory they would obtain over the Philistines.

If you are at a crossroads in your life, if the Lord has spoken to you and told you to do something outside of your comfort zone, there is no sin in asking the Lord to confirm what He has told you. It's one thing to venture out halfheartedly thinking we heard the voice of the Lord, it's another to venture out wholly committed to the task at hand because we know the Lord has spoken to us.

It is a dangerous thing to be plagued by uncertainty, fear, or doubt when set upon a task and purpose meant to further the kingdom of God.

No matter how faithful one might be, if one is uncertain or doubtful in regards to having heard from God, there will be hesitation in their decisions, second guessing, and often times even a paralyzing fear.

Few feelings in life are worse than finding ourselves far from everything we've ever known, separated from friends and family alike, and wondering whether or not this was the will of God for our lives, or if we talked ourselves into believing something concerning which we are now doubtful and skeptical. Whatever the task, whether great or small, confirm and reconfirm, until you are at peace, and know it was the voice of God you heard, and it was God who commissioned you to set about a certain course.

David wanted to make sure the Lord had said what He had said. David wanted to be certain it was not his own ego driving him to war against the Philistines, but rather the Lord. Once he was certain, David and his men struck a mighty blow to the Philistines, and saved the inhabitants of Keilah.

What David confirms time and again is that prayer is dialogue; prayer is communication. If David was uncertain concerning something in his life, he went to the Lord in prayer, and the Lord answered him.

David spoke to God as to a Master, and a Father, a Lord, and a friend.

> Samuel 23:10-12, "Then David said, 'O Lord God of Israel, Your servant has certainly heard that Saul seeks to come to Keilah to destroy the city for my sake. Will the men of Keilah deliver me into his hand? Will Saul come down, as Your servant has heard? O Lord God of Israel, I pray, tell Your servant.' And the Lord said, 'He will come down.' Then David said, 'Will the men of Keilah deliver me and my men into the hand of Saul?' and the Lord said, 'They will deliver you.'"

Just in these three verses alone we see the specificity of David's questions concerning his immediate future, and the specificity of God's answers. Even though he had just saved the men of Keilah from the hands of the Philistines, David inquires of the Lord as to whether or not they would betray him and deliver him into the hands of Saul, and God's answer is that they will.

Instead of trying to convince God as to why the men of Keilah wouldn't betray him, David and his men arose and departed Keilah and went wherever they could. It is often God tells us a difficult thing, a hard thing, but nevertheless a true thing. We believe what God tells us not because it feels good, or because we necessarily want to, but because we have to. David didn't want to hear he would be betrayed by the men of Keilah. He didn't want to believe that after saving them from the hands of the Philistines, risking his own life in the process, these men would turn on him, betray him, and deliver him to Saul.

Because God told him it would be thus, David believed God at His Word, and without delay departed Keilah with all his men.

I've only had it happen once, but in truth, once is all that's necessary for anyone to never again delay, or doubt the words of God.

Some years ago, I was in a prayer meeting and a word came forth warning that one close to me would betray me. Although I believed the word, I didn't act upon it and the person I suspected of being the betrayer never gave any indication of his plans. Some time passed, and as time is wont to do, the urgency of the word I received was dulled. I'd almost forgotten the prophecy I'd received when the fateful day arrived, and the person of whom the word of the Lord had warned, tried in the most vicious, cunning, and heartless way to destroy the work, the ministry, and members of my family.

Could I have prevented this from happening? Probably not, but if I had been wiser, I could have prepared in such a way that when the word came to pass, I would have been ready to confront the individual head on. That was the one and only time I took a word from the Lord lightly, or failed to act upon it immediately. In His love God warns us, He speaks to us, He counsels us, but we still have to choose to take action, and obey the leading of the Lord.

Chances are good both David and his men were tired from having fought the Philistines. All they really wanted was to rest awhile, to eat, perhaps to sleep, then figure out what they would do if Saul decided to come up to Keilah. It is likely some of David's men grumbled at the thought of having to leave Keilah, tired, bruised, and hungry, but God had spoken, and David was wise enough to heed the counsel of the Lord and follow through.

Many times, the promises of God are not fulfilled in our lives, because we did not follow through with what He commanded of us.

If God tells us to go minister in a certain place, and He would show great signs and stir the hearts of many to repentance, if we fail to go, if we fail to obey, then we cannot expect him to fulfill the promise of stirring hearts and showing great signs. The signs and the stirring of the hearts were contingent upon us going. If we fail to obey, then God cannot fulfill the rest of His promise toward us.

Something strange happens in the hearts of men when they don't follow through with what God has instructed, and when, as consequence, God doesn't follow through with what He promised. Rather than search their hearts to see why God's promises have not come to fruition, they grow bitter and resentful toward God for not following through.

There are certain promises God makes which are contingent upon the obedience, steadfastness, and faithfulness of the individual. If the individual in question does not obey, if they get distracted, or otherwise sidetracked, God simply finds another vessel through which to perform the works He promised, and carry out His will.

God is not dependent upon us, we are dependent upon God. No man—no matter how great the calling on their life or the gifting in which they operated—is indispensable. God will not overlook sin, disobedience, rebellion, or duplicity in the heart of an individual no matter how gifted they might be, because God would rather not do a thing, than have the thing He desired to do be tainted.

God is a holy God, he is a righteous God, and it is in righteousness and holiness He performs and brings to pass His will in the lives of obedient and humble servants. 'David inquired of the Lord' this was the pattern of his life, and after inquiring of the Lord, and receiving the answer to his query, David acted on the information he'd received without delay.

Although a flawed man, David never once assumed he knew better than God, or thought himself above the correction of God. When our desire is to walk in the will of God, we inquire of Him. When our desire is to do as God would have us do, we receive His counsel and act upon his directives.

One of the worst things we can do is take God's counsel under advisement. I've heard this term from the lips of men who I assumed knew better than to tempt the Lord their God by inquiring of Him, then discounting and ignoring His words in lieu of their own notions, opinions, or plans. If your heart is set upon something, and you have no desire to do as God commands but as you see fit, don't tempt the Lord by inquiring of Him. Inquire of the Lord only when you are ready to obey, to upturn your entire life, and walk away from everything you have meticulously built thus far. If you are not ready to obey completely, then there's no point in inquiring of the Lord.

'Lord, lead me and I will follow, but don't ask me to quit my job, leave my city, have contact with homeless people, or give more than ten percent after taxes.'

What's the point? Why even pray the prayer?

If we start out by telling God what we're not willing to do for Him, then our first priority ought to be getting our hearts right, then asking Him to assign us a task or duty. I do what I do because God commanded it of me. If He tells me to keep going, I keep going. If He tells me to stop, I stop. And if He tells me to walk away from it all, I won't even take the time to pack a bag.

True obedience obeys even when what is asked of us is in our detriment, when it hurts the flesh, when it wounds our pride, and when, in the eyes of the world it sets us back rather than moves us forward. Before bending our knee or uttering the first words of a prayer, we must be prepared to receive an answer our flesh will not like or bristle against. Not every answer we receive from the Lord will be positive, or joyous. Sometimes God asks us to do the hard thing, the difficult thing, the thing we most don't want to do, and as obedient children we must lay aside our preferences, and do as commanded.

If every believer made at a habit to inquire of the Lord with consistency, there would be many a giant of the faith walking about today, full of the presence, power and authority of God. When we inquire of the Lord we are submitting to His authority over us, and humbling ourselves to the point of following His guidance for our lives.

Instead of inquiring of the Lord, nowadays most believers think themselves little gods, and being little gods–at least in their own minds–they are able to justify the path they choose to follow, no matter how far removed from the truth of Scripture it might be. There are times when God will not answer though we inquire of Him. Like David, Saul was disciplined in regards to inquiring of the Lord. Even after he rebelled, disobeyed, and did what God had commanded him not to do, Saul continued to inquire of the Lord, but the Lord did not answer His queries.

Saul spoke, but God was silent. Saul inquired, but God did not answer, because a wall had been erected between God and Saul, a wall of disobedience and rebellion which God could not overlook.

When Saul saw God would not answer, he even went to the prophet of the Lord, asking him to inquire of God on his behalf, but it was too late by far. God had already rejected Saul from being king, and had chosen another to take his place. Due to their lack of relationship with Him, God will not allow Himself to be inquired of by certain people, even if they attempt to use surrogates to do so. Take Ezekiel for example.

Ezekiel 20:1-3, "It came to pass in the seventh year, in the fifth month, on the tenth day of the month, that certain of the elders of Israel came to inquire of the Lord, and sat before me. Then the word of the Lord came to me, saying, 'Son of man, speak to the elders of Israel, and say to them, 'thus says the Lord God: 'Have you come to inquire of Me? As I live,' says the Lord God, 'I will not be inquired of by you.'"

The elders of Israel had come to Ezekiel inquiring of the Lord, but the Lord's only answer was that He would not be inquired of by them. Even though they attempted to use Ezekiel as a conduit, as an intermediary between themselves and God, God saw through it and rebuked them for having the gall to come inquire of Him without first removing the abominations and idols from before their eyes.

If we inquire of the Lord and He does not answer, it is paramount we search our hearts, repent of what our conscience convicts us of, and then inquire of the Lord again. God has good reason for not answering our query and it is never that He was busy, on vacation, doing something else, or overwhelmed by all the prayers.

Diligent study of the Scriptures reveals it is man not being in harmony with God and His will that keeps Him from answering when we inquire of Him. God's hand is not short, His hearing is not impaired, and He is not shortsighted. If fault lies with anyone, it is with us, and once we patch the rift, and return to walking in His will, He will answer our petitions.

When we know and trust God, we can't help but inquire of Him. Each time Israel did not inquire of the Lord regarding something it always ended up being to their detriment. Even when they thought they were getting the good end of the deal, when it was all added up and the final tally was done, they were still at a loss.

God has a better vantage point than we do. He sees beyond what we can see, and if something seems good to us, but seems bad to God, trust that God can see farther down the line than you, and can better ascertain whether the experience will end up being a positive or negative one.

Isaiah 30:1, "Woe to the rebellious children,' says the Lord, 'who take counsel but not of Me, and who devise plans but not of My Spirit, that they may add sin to sin.'"

God's desire is that we take counsel of Him, and make plans by His Spirit. Only when we are dependent on His guidance, can we be certain of our destination, and know the path upon which we are walking is according to His will.

David inquired of the Lord whenever he needed to make a decision, and if he had inquired of the Lord in other areas of his life, perhaps there would be no blemish to speak of on his journey.

It matters not how wise your human counselors might be, it matters not how good the advice you received from friends or family is, God always knows best. Even if God's counsel stands in stark opposition to the counsel of those you trust do as God instructs, and you will see the benefit and wisdom of doing what God commands sooner rather than later.

From David we learn time and again that prayer is dialogue with God. Because of what prayer is, it ought not to be cumbersome to us, nor ought we to view prayer as a chore. Prayer is a privilege, an honor, and a grace which we, the children of God are given, and understanding the beauty of what prayer was, David was consistent in being in God's presence and inquiring of Him.

There are times when not inquiring of God leads to lifelong consequences. Whether to sell one's home in lieu of a nicer one, to quit one's job for the promise of a better one, to marry or not to marry, when we make such decisions without inquiring of God, if we make the wrong choice, the consequences of our singular action can stretch on for decades.

It is the epitome of foolishness to trust in our own wisdom, when the source of all wisdom stands ready to counsel us, and answer our queries. It would be something wholly different if we had no one to run to, if we had no one to inquire of, if we were left on this rock all by ourselves with no hope, no future, and no direction, but God is listening, and His heart desires fellowship with His creation. Failing to inquire of the Lord can be likened to attempting to write a sonnet, having Shakespeare standing next to you, and not bothering to ask his advice.

God knows best, He always has, He always will, and if we want the best for our lives, then we must humble ourselves, admit we don't know it all, and inquire of Him as to what course to take and what path to follow.

Perhaps it was the volume of time David spent in the presence of the Lord, and how often he inquired of the Lord that elevated his prayers to something akin to poetry. Not only did David inquire of the Lord often and with regularity, the words he used in his prayers, and the way in which he praised and magnified God, are wondrously beautiful.

David was a man of action, but he was also a man of words. Having written over half of the psalms included in the Book of Psalms, his tender heart toward God is revealed time and again. When he sinned, he was quick to humble himself into the dust, and repent before God, but when God showed him favor, David was also quick to bow before the Lord and bring prayers of thanks before Him.

In this, we have another practical lesson we must learn from the life of David. From David's life we learn to spend time in the presence of God not only when we need to repent of something, petition God for something, or intercede on behalf of someone, but also when He has been good to us, when He has blessed us, and when He has shown us favor.

Seeing as every breath is a gift, and every sunrise and sunset a reason to thank the Lord, seeing as every meal, every article of clothing and the fact we have a roof over our heads is all due to Him, we ought not to allow a single day to go by without thanking Him for His many blessings.

David had learned the art of being thankful to God for all things. Even after being anointed king, David did not forget his small and meager beginnings. He did not forget he had been a sheepherder, and every grace God showed him, every favor bestowed upon him, was a reason to be thankful to God and in awe of Him. As wise children, we must be in awe of God's grace and favor toward us every day of our lives. We can take nothing for granted, or assume we're entitled to anything. Everything from our health, to our spouses, to our children, to our homes, to our jobs are a gift from the hand of God, and we must treat them as such.

Having seen the abundance of blessing God had bestowed upon him, David decides to build a house for the ark of God. He shares his heart with the prophet Nathan, and before Nathan could ask God if this was His will, he speaks to David and says, 'go, do all that is in your heart, for the Lord is with you.'

I know not why Nathan did not inquire of the Lord whether David ought to build a house for the ark or not, but alas, that night the word of the Lord came to Nathan and commanded him to go and tell God's servant David that he would not be the one building him a house, but his seed would. Even the best of intentions can have the wrong outcome if they are not the will of God. Perhaps it was because it seemed like such a good idea, that Nathan did not inquire of the Lord as to whether or not David ought to build a house for the ark. It was a noble gesture, a good thing, what could be wrong in something so selfless?

One of the most difficult lessons for us to learn as human beings is that the purpose of our existence on this earth is not to be magnanimous, charitable, giving, or generous for the sake of it, but because we are acting out our obedience toward God. The purpose of our existence is obedience and walking in the will of God. And yes, oftentimes God calls us to be benevolent and altruistic.

God rewards obedience. This truth has been proven out in Scripture time and again. If I want to do something noble and kind yet God tells me not to do it at that particular time, if I follow through and do what I proposed to do, even though it was a noble thing, I would still be in rebellion and disobedience toward God.

Sometimes obedience is the easiest thing in the world, at other times the most difficult. When, what God commands us goes against the grain of our preconceived notions and ideas, the humbling of oneself is required in order to lay aside our wants, our wills, and simply obey.

David knew there was no point in arguing with God, and the promise God made David concerning the house his seed would build for the Lord, caused him to bend his knee and pray one of the most beautiful prayers of the Old Testament.

> *2 Samuel 7:18-22, "Then King David went in and sat before the Lord; and he said, 'Who am I, O Lord God? And what is my house, that You have brought me this far? And yet this was a small thing in Your sight, O Lord God; and You have also spoken of Your servant's house for a great while to come. Is this the manner of man, O Lord God? Now what more can David say to You? For You, Lord God, know Your servant. For Your word's sake, and according to Your own heart, You have done all these great things, to make Your servant know them. Therefore You are great, O Lord God. For there is none like You, nor is there any God besides You, according to all that we have heard with our ears.'"*

Although David's prayer continues for another seven verses, I would be remiss if I did not point out some evident truths from his prayer thus far.

The first thing to stand out is David's genuine humility. Although he had been anointed king, David stands before God and asks, 'Who am I, O Lord God? And what is my house, that you have brought me this far?'

If we begin to juxtapose David's prayer with the prayers of any given televangelist nowadays, we begin to see the stark difference between the two. Though David was king, he still inquired of the Lord 'who am I, O Lord?' while men with an iota of tenuous power and influence scream of their entitlement to the heavens, reminding God that they too are little gods and ought to be appeased. There is a great difference between 'Lord I am unworthy of your many blessings,' and 'is this all you're going to give me Lord? I deserve more! In fact, I'm entitled to more!' In recent years we have consistently moved away from godliness with contentment, and toward the mentality that God somehow owes us, and if we demand it loudly enough, often enough, and sternly enough, He will do as we demand.

David understood what many today choose not to: that God's blessings are undeserved and when He chooses to bless us, all we can do is thank Him for His goodness and faithfulness.

The second thing to stand out in David's prayer is his unshakable faith in the promises of God. God had spoken some great things to David through the prophet Nathan, including that his house and kingdom would be established forever before him. At the time of this prophecy, David still had enemies who were all around, there was still division among his own people, yet when God spoke, David believed God at His word and began to thank Him for all the great things He had done. In David's heart the matter was already settled, and God had already done these great things.

The third thing to stand out in David's prayer is his awareness of God's greatness. 'There is none like You, nor is there any God beside You,' David says. It's not just the words David spoke, but what they imply that's of true import. David acknowledged the supremacy of God, the uniqueness of God, and the omnipotence of God. David knew the God he served, knew the extent of His power, the wonder of His majesty, and because he knew God, he stood on the promises of God accepting them as having already been made manifest.

There was no doubt in David's heart concerning the greatness of the God he served. Even in his darkest hour, standing against his most imposing foe, David knew God was with him, and if God was with him, then any foe, no matter how imposing, was as good as felled already. David knew with whom he was communing. David possessed the requisite reverence, any man understanding who it is they are speaking to, must possess.

Rather than be in awe of His greatness, we continually attempt to bring God down to our level, remaking Him in an image more to our liking, instead of allowing ourselves to be remolded into an image more akin to Him. Due to this, we lose awareness of the One to whom we are speaking when we pray, at least not as far as His majesty and greatness are concerned. The proof is in the lack of reverence which seems to permeate nearly every congregation or household of faith.

We have redefined God, and we have shrunk His authority, His majesty, and His omnipotence, to the point of utter irreverence for His holy name. Rather than come before Him in a spirit of worship and reverence, many today approach God as know-it-all bratty children who just want to be validated in their choices, their lifestyle, and their predilections. 'God is whatever you want Him to be, but in general, he's like your buddy, you know, your pal, someone you can joke around with and stuff.'

Since when is God our buddy and our pal? When was it He stripped Himself of His sovereignty, majesty, righteousness, holiness, omnipotence and divinity and become someone we can joke around with? We read David's words, and we realize He revered God. David had reverence for whom God was and acknowledged his own impotence and inferiority in light of whom God was. When reverence is lacking, so is everything else necessary to ensure a true relationship with God. From humility, to subservience, to obedience, to faith itself, all these things are absent when reverence is absent in the heart of an individual.

Due to lack of reverence, we also have the disastrous tendency to reinterpret and redefine God by our own standards. When we do this, our go to response is, 'my god wouldn't do that,' whenever something we don't understand or like occurs.

But is that the God of the Bible? If we read the Book and see God doing a certain thing or taking a certain action yet we do not believe our god would do the selfsame thing, we are not worshipping the God of the Bible, but a god of our own making. David didn't try to change God, he submitted to God's authority and sovereignty, receiving all things from His hand.

Granted, it's easy to receive from the hand of God when what He is promising you is the continuity of your kingdom and perpetual protection, but there were times when God tested David in ways that might seem harsh or unloving to us, yet David still humbled himself in the sight of the Lord. Is reverence or respect an option rather than a necessity for the children of God? Can we choose irreverence absent consequence – as some insist – if we so desire?

Revelation 4:9-11, "Whenever the living creatures give glory and honor and thanks to Him who sits on the throne, who lives forever and ever, the twenty-four elders fall down before Him who sits on the throne and worship Him who lives forever and ever, and cast their crowns before the throne, saying: 'You are worthy, O Lord, to receive glory and honor and power, for You created all things, and by Your will they exist and were created.'"

If in heaven there is reverence and worship of God to the point that the twenty-four elders fall down before Him, and cast their crowns before the throne, and if with our own lips we pray, 'Your kingdom come, Your will be done on earth as it is in heaven,' then ought we not to show the same reverence as those in heaven do?

He is Lord! He is God! He is Creator! He is worthy of our reverence, and worship.

Though David was king and people feared him, since with the wave of a hand he could have the life of any man in his kingdom, he humbled himself in the sight of the Lord, recognizing His authority, and His lordship over his life. To some this topic may seem like a small issue, or a non-issue, but I assure you lack of reverence leads to lack of obedience, which leads to lack of accountability, which is the first step in the downward spiral of rebellion.

Fools will beat their chest and say 'I am,' but wise men bow their knee and say, 'You are!'

'Who am I, O Lord God? And what is my house, that You have brought me this far?' These were the first words of David's prayer, and no, he had not been stricken with sudden Alzheimer's. David knew who he was as a person, he knew who he was as far as his position was concerned, but he still could not fathom what God saw in him that he had been elevated to such a state. David humbled himself in the sight of the Lord, and revered God's ability to take a lump of clay and mold greatness out of it.

If you have accomplished anything in this life, if you are someone of renown, keep in mind it was God who brought you this far. It was the hand of God which led you and molded you and carried you to this place. Give God the thanks and glory rightly His, as David did so long ago. A lesser man would have attempted to appropriate the glory for himself. It was after all David who pitched the stone at Goliath's head, it was David who led his army to victory, but David knew that though his hand pitched the stone, God guided it. Though David led his armies, God gave the victory.

Human arrogance and the pride of life must disappear like fog in the sunlight when we stand before God. One cannot know God, yet be arrogant before Him. One cannot know God, and retain pride in their individual accomplishments or aptitudes.

We cannot be in the presence of the one true God, and still see ourselves as great, because his greatness highlights our own insignificance. When confronted with God's holiness, we see our own unworthiness, and realize it is only by the blood of Christ that we are able to enter in, and be partakers of His holiness.

Matthew 8:5-8, "Now when Jesus had entered Capernaum, a centurion came to Him, pleading with Him, saying, 'Lord, my servant is lying at home paralyzed, dreadfully tormented.' And Jesus said to him, 'I will come and heal him.' The centurion answered and said, 'Lord, I am not worthy that You should come under my roof. But only speak a word, and my servant will be healed.'"

In order to understand what had just taken place in this passage, we must first understand who this centurion was, and what his role was during the days of Jesus.

During the period of time Jesus walked the earth, the whole of Israel was under Roman rule. The Roman Empire had stretched itself far and wide, and the Romans of the day had autonomy as well as much power throughout the land. The man who came to Jesus was a centurion. He was not just an enlisted man, nor was he someone of no renown. A centurion was in charge of a one hundred man garrison, someone respected within the construct of the Roman political system, and someone to whom others deferred.

The Romans of the time considered every other nationality or race beneath them, so for this centurion to say he was not worthy of Christ coming under his roof, meant a true humbling of the self, and the subjugation of the arrogance for which Romans as a people were known for.

I realize we like to think of ourselves as great and grand specimens of intelligence and wisdom, but in reality, God doesn't need a lot to work with to make something remarkable.

Yes, that stings, especially the pride we harbor in our hearts, but God didn't test my IQ before calling me into the ministry, He didn't put me through a physical to see if my heart could handle the strain, He didn't ask to see my wardrobe to decide whether I had enough suits, He called and I answered.

A potter just needs clay. Even the most beautiful and prized pieces of art start out as lumps of clay. It's not about the clay. Clay is clay. It's about the proficiency of the potter, and what he can do with the lump of clay in his hands. It's not about my aptitude, my intelligence quotient, or my abilities as a public speaker; it's about what God can do through me.

Because it is about God's ability and not our own, all that is incumbent upon us to do is submit, and not resist the molding and chiseling of the Lord. The potter knows what the piece of clay will look like when he's done with it, and God knows what you will look like when He's done with you.

Even though the promise of something beautiful is ever present in the Word of God, even though we know He is a good God who desires only our sanctification, we often find ourselves resisting His correction, His molding and His chiseling. It is to our detriment when we allow pride to override humility, and when we allow arrogance to override obedience.

When we acknowledge our own limitations, we give God the glory for everything He does through us. If we are honest with ourselves we know where we end and He begins. We know the true measure of our wit and knowledge, we know the true measure of our strength and ability, and each time we see ourselves surpassing our own limitations, we must give God the glory, for it is He who is doing a work through us.

David was a man who knew his limitations, and acknowledged the blessing and grace of God over his life all of his days. David knew God knew him completely, so there was no pretense in David. David did not try to project an image contrary to who he really was; he didn't try to seem more righteous than God knew him to be, because David acknowledged God's intimate knowledge of him.

'Now what more can David say to You? For You, Lord God, know Your servant.'

When we know God knows us, pride, arrogance and self, wither and die. One cannot maintain an attitude of arrogance and pride knowing that they are an open book in the sight of God. One cannot put the self upon a pedestal, when they realize God knows everything, from the moment we breathed our first breath, to the moment we will breathe our last.

God knows of our inconsistency, He knows of our doubt, He knows of our hardened heart, He knows of our indifference, He knows of our omissions, and only one who knows not God as they ought can still stand before Him shrouded in self.

Psalm 139:1-4, "O Lord, You have searched me and know me. You know my sitting down and my rising up; You understand my thought afar off. You comprehend my path and my lying down, and are acquainted with all my ways. For there is not a word on my tongue, but behold, O Lord, You know it altogether."

God knows His servants. Not tangentially, or partially, but wholly, fully and completely. He knows you, He understands your thought, He comprehends your path, and is acquainted with all your ways.

Knowledge is reciprocal in nature. I cannot know someone intimately without them knowing me as well. I cannot claim to know my wife, for example, without my wife also knowing me. God knew David, but by the wording of his prayer we realize David likewise knew God. David begins to list the attributes of God, and glory in His majesty to such an extent, that we begin to realize the depth David had accumulated in God over the years.

Getting to know God is a progressive journey. One cannot wake up one morning and know God in the fullness of His majesty, but we can grow in God on a daily basis, and have the nature of God crystalize before us, becoming all the more vivid. In his prayer David also acknowledges the tenderness of God's heart, and His predisposition to blessing His servants.

'For Your Word's sake, and according to Your own heart, You have done all these great things, to make Your servant know them.'

David realized it was not because he deserved it, but for God's Word's sake, and according to His heart, He does these great things on his behalf. Even in the most dire of circumstances we must not forget God's tender heart toward us.

'Therefore You are great, O Lord God. For there is none like You, nor is there any God besides You, according to all that we have heard with our ears.'

When was the last time you glorified the Lord for His greatness like David? When was the last time you stood before God, with reverence and in awe, and said, 'You are great Lord, there is none like You, nor is there any God beside You'?

Do we only come before God when we have a need? Do we approach Him only when we have a problem, when we need a breakthrough, a healing, or a financial outpouring, or do we regularly bow before Him just to praise His name? If men know when they are being taken advantage of, God knows as well. There are many calling themselves sons and daughters of God, whose only interaction with God comes about when they need something from Him.

Even though God's heart is tender, even though according to His own heart He does great things for us, He doesn't like being used, or taken advantage of. David knew God as redeemer. As the one who had redeemed for Himself a people, and in his epic prayer, David also acknowledged the redemption of God, for himself as well as the people of Israel.

> 2 Samuel 7:23-24, "And who is like Your people, like Israel, the one nation on the earth whom God went to redeem for Himself as a people, to make for Himself a name – and to do for You great and awesome deeds for Your land – before Your people whom You redeemed for Yourself from Egypt, from the nations and their gods. For You have made Your people Israel Your very own people forever; and You, Lord, have become their God."

David's understanding of God's intent, as well as God's promises is second to none, and in his prayer he is able to articulate not only the majesty and greatness of God, but the plan of God for himself and the nation of Israel. David declares unashamedly that the Lord is the God of the people. Given today's attempts at making one's faith as vague as possible, it is refreshing to read the words of David and realize his declaration left no room for wondering whether or not Israel was the people of God.

Not only does David declare that the Lord is Israel's God, both unequivocally and unashamedly, he also declares the entire nation's dependency upon God. David acknowledges God as having been the one to have made His people, and he does not attempt to minimize God's involvement or highlight his own contribution. All glory is given to God.

If we do not have power, it is because we have distanced ourselves from the source of power. If we do not have victory, it is because we trust in ourselves to obtain the victory rather than trust God to make us victorious. David knew the smaller he became in his own eyes and the greater God became to him, the more the presence and guidance of God would be evident in his life as well as that of his nation.

When we humble ourselves in the sight of the Lord as David did, it is God who lifts us up, and when God lifts us up we defer all glory and praise to Him, realizing it as His doing and not our own. David praises God because he realizes, in and of himself, he would still be shepherding his father's sheep, unknown to anyone but those closest to him, a once simple boy who grew to be a simple man, from a family of little renown. He likewise realizes it is the Lord who will have to keep him standing lest he fall by the wayside. David knows that try as he might to continue his house, if the Lord does not intervene and work on his behalf, it will not be so. He has no illusions about his abilities, and lays it all at the Lord's feet, petitioning Him to continue blessing his house as He promised.

2 Samuel 7:29, "Now therefore, let it please You to bless the house of your servant, that it may continue forever before You; for You, O Lord God, have spoken it, and with Your blessing let the house of Your servant be blessed forever."

Acknowledge the blessing of God over your life, acknowledge that He alone has brought you thus far, and you will live under the shadow of His wing, kept safe in His embrace. Although humility has become anathema in many a Christian circles, it is still something God honors, and when we humble ourselves before Him, He will raise us up to where He desires us to be.

David's life was neither linear, nor in perpetual ascent. There were moments in David's life wherein he allowed the flesh to overwhelm the spirit, wherein he did not pray and seek the face of the Lord, but did as he desired.

Since we've discussed David's first recorded prayer and his prayer after being told of the blessings God would bestow upon him and his household, I want to continue our discussion of David's prayer life with a prayer he prayed after he was rebuked by the selfsame prophet who had previously come to tell David of God's favor upon him.

David had strayed. He had allowed the lust of his eyes to dictate his actions, and had orchestrated the death of a man named Uriah in order to claim his widow Bathsheba. This was the low point of David's walk, and the Lord sent Nathan the prophet to David in order to rebuke him. To aid in opening David's eyes to the enormity of his sin, Nathan spoke a parable of a rich man and a poor man to him.

Both the rich man and the poor man lived in the same city, and while the rich man was exceedingly wealthy, the poor man had nothing except one little ewe lamb which he had bought and nourished. The poor man loved his lamb to the extent that it ate of his own food, drank from his own cup, and lay in his bosom. As it happened, a traveler came to the rich man, and refusing to take from his own flock in order to prepare a meal for the traveler, he took the poor man's lamb and prepared it for the man who had come to him.

2 Samuel 12:5-6, "Then David's anger was greatly aroused against the man, and he said to Nathan, 'As the Lord lives the man who has done this shall surely die! And he shall restore fourfold for the lamb, because he did this thing and because he had no pity.'"

If Nathan would have come right out and accused David of being an adulterer, and one who plotted the murder of his own man, perhaps David would have attempted to justify his actions, or minimize his accountability in the matter. Because Nathan started out with the parable of a nondescript, faceless, and unknown 'rich man' and described what David had done using the ewe lamb as an example, David's anger was greatly aroused against the man, though he did not know him, because his actions were inexcusable, despicable, and immoral.

2 Samuel 12:7-9, "Then Nathan said to David, 'You are the man! Thus says the Lord God of Israel: 'I anointed you king over Israel, and I delivered you from the hand of Saul. I gave you your master's house and your master's wives into your keeping, and gave you the house of Israel and Judah. And if they had been too little, I also would have given you much more! Why have you despised the commandment of the Lord, to do evil in His sight? You have killed Uriah the Hittite with the sword; you have taken his wife to be your wife, and have killed him with the sword of the people of Ammon.'"

Imagine someone telling you the story of a heartless individual, who was cruel, and merciless, and who did vile things. Then imagine, once the story is done, and you are thoroughly angered, the individual telling you the story delivers the punch line: 'You are the man!'

If I were to venture a guess as to how David felt when he heard these four words, I would say he felt a lot like one feels when they're on a plane, and the plane hits an air pocket. David's stomach likely rose in his throat, and he felt as though he was falling, not sure if the fall would ever stop. One instant he is ready to put the man in Nathan's parable to death, the next instant he discovers he is the man of whom the prophet spoke.

Not only did Nathan reveal David's sin to him, he also revealed why it was so egregious in the sight of God. God judged David's sin on its face, but also in light of how much blessing God had bestowed upon him, and how much favor He had shown him throughout his life. Although David did not strike the blow, but had Uriah–the man he is accused of killing–placed where the battle was thickest then instructed his men to withdraw, God still concluded it was David who killed him.

The words spoken by Nathan were harsh words to be sure, and through him God inquires of David why it was he chose to despise the commandments of the Lord, and do evil in His sight. If this would have happened in our modern age, perhaps the answer to God's query might have been, 'because it felt good, because sin is relative, because the preacher told me I'm saved, sealed, and sanctified forever no matter what I do,' but David's answer was one of admission, confession, and taking responsibility for what he had done.

2 Samuel 12:13-14, "Then David said to Nathan, 'I have sinned against the Lord.' And Nathan said to David, 'The Lord also has put away your sin; you shall not die. However, because by this deed you have given great occasion to the enemies of the Lord to blaspheme, the child also who is born to you shall surely die.'"

There is no sin without consequence, not the least of which is giving great occasion to the enemies of the Lord to blaspheme. We live neither in a bubble, nor in a vacuum. Men see us every day, they see our actions, they see our conduct, they see our lifestyle, and Lord forbid that we give them occasion to blaspheme as David did. Sin is the ruin of individuals, families, cities and nations. Wherever sin is given free reign, it corrupts, erodes, and destroys, for it is in its nature to do so. One cannot reason with sin, nor can one reach an armistice with it, because other than to destroy, sin has no desire or aspiration.

You cannot bribe sin, you cannot hide sin, all one can do is pluck sin from its roots, and toss into the fire. Sinning less is not an option or a remedy. At best, sinning less is a lull, and at worst it is a self-delusion created to soothe the burdened conscience. David did not try to excuse, justify, or shy away from the truth. 'I have sinned against the Lord.' This was both a declarative statement, and an admission of guilt. It was a full confession, without attempting to first strike a deal, or to get a more lenient punishment.

David was in the wrong, he knew he was in the wrong, and he confessed to being in the wrong. He had sinned, he knew he had sinned, and he realized trying to obfuscate the situation or mitigate his guilt would only stir the wrath of God. Sin is ever lurking in the shadows; it is always watching, and waiting, hoping for an in, hoping for a moment of weakness, a temporary lapse in judgment, an instant of distraction wherein we are not watchful or are weary.

David's life shows us the need for vigilance, because we see even praying men can sin, even humble men can sin, even men after God's own heart can sin, if they are not watchful and guarded in regards to their heart. We are on a journey, and the final destination of this journey is glory. Along the way the hosts of hell will do everything in their power to distract us, cause us to veer off the path, or keep us from progressing any further. We begin this journey fully aware of the opposition we face, fully aware of our own limitations, but also fully confident in the knowledge that Jesus is with us every step of the way.

The devil does not fear me, he fears He who is in me. The devil does not fear you, he fears the Christ in you, and this knowledge must birth in us a true and lasting humility and dependency upon Him.

David knew better. We see it in his prayers, we see it in his devotion, but rather than pluck temptation from his heart, he allowed it to take root and grow until David rationalized both despising the commandment of the Lord, and doing evil in His sight.

Matthew 26:41, "Watch and pray, lest you enter into temptation. The spirit indeed is willing but the flesh is weak."

David thought himself invincible. Somewhere along the way David stopped watching, and he stopped praying and once this occurred it was only a matter of time before sin felled him. For a season David even pretended as though what he had done was acceptable, or justifiable, until the fateful day when the prophet of God came to challenge him. It was only after the prophet Nathan confronted him and opened his eyes to the reality of what he had done that David confessed his sin against the Lord.

If the children of God viewed sin as God Himself views sin, there would be a lot less sin within the household of faith. David sinned, and his entire trajectory changed. He was no longer on the path God had outlined for him. In essence, the entire purpose of sin is to keep you from reaching the destination God had in mind for you. When we sin, we deviate from the plan of God for our lives, and become our own worst enemies. David saw where his doing evil in the sight of God was leading him. He realized he had lost his joy because of his sin, and rather than attempt to hide what he had done, he confessed his sin before the Lord.

For some the act of confessing one's sins is difficult. Confessing our sins before God implies wrongdoing and failure on our part, and for many a soul admitting they were wrong is hard. As hard as is confessing one's sins and accepting responsibility for what we do, it is harder still to live with a sin of which we have not repented.

Psalm 32:3-5, "When I kept silent my bones grew old through my groaning all day long. For day and night Your hand was heavy upon me; my vitality was turned into the drought of summer. Selah. I acknowledged my sin to You, and my iniquity I have not hidden. I said, 'I will confess my transgressions to the Lord,' and you forgave the iniquity of my sin. Selah."

The same man who stood before the Lord confessing his sin, now confesses how horrible it was not acknowledging his sin to God. His bones grew old, his vitality disappeared, and the hand of the Lord was heavy upon him, all because he did not confess his transgressions to the Lord. It is a sad thing when we allow stubbornness and pride to dictate our spiritual decisions.

Countless souls talk themselves into believing that it's easier to pretend and feign holiness, than to confess their transgressions before the Lord and truly be forgiven. As is often the case, if we tell ourselves a lie often enough we start to believe it, and the men and women of which I speak have come to believe that all they really need to do is pretend well enough to enter heaven.

There is only one antidote to sin, there is only one thing men can do in order to alleviate the pain and hopelessness sin brings about in a life, and that is to repent. Acknowledge what God already knows, confess your transgression to the Lord, that He might forgive the iniquity of your sin. There is no point in attempting to excuse sin in our lives, or to mitigate our responsibility and participation. God knows, and the only thing which compels Him to forgive the iniquity of our sins is to come before Him in humility, confess, and repent.

As children of God we should have an aversion to sin.

Some years ago I was sitting in a breakfast diner minding my own business and enjoying an omelet, when two tables away from me someone started coughing loudly, and banging the table. I lifted my head and saw a middle aged couple with breakfasts of their own in front of them, and what, I assumed, was the husband making the ruckus.

In no time the man started wheezing violently, his face turned bright red, and his female companion became distraught herself and stared screaming for someone to call an ambulance.

The man was still clinging to the table, barely breathing by the time the ambulance came, and in a distraught voice the woman informed the emergency medical technician of the severe peanut allergy the man suffered from. The man almost died because he accidentally ingested something he was allergic to. We must view sin in much the same terms. Sin is not something God winks at, sweeps under the rug, or ignores in our lives. Sin kills. Sin is as deadly for a believer, as the crushed peanuts were in the batter of the waffle the man was eating before he had his attack.

When we minimize the destructive power of sin, we tend to flirt with it more than we ought. When we acknowledge how devastating it is for both individuals, families and communities alike, we stay away from it, and do our utmost to avoid it. In his instruction for holy living to the church of Thessalonica, Paul simply says, 'abstain from every form of evil.' Simple, direct, and unequivocal! Paul doesn't qualify his statement by saying some forms of evil are more acceptable than others, he does not say we should abstain on from certain kinds of evil, but from every form of evil.

Yes, we must abstain from every form of evil. To abstain is to restrain oneself from doing or enjoying something. It is making the conscious decision to say 'no,' when saying 'yes,' would be momentarily more pleasurable to the flesh. A fleeting pleasure hides lifelong consequences. We see this reality played out time and again with every generation, yet rather than learn from the mistakes of those who came before them, every generation seems to be quickening its pace toward the edge of the precipice.

David's sin did not go unpunished. Even though he confessed his transgression before God, there was still a price to be paid for the sin he committed. Though God may forgive the sinful act, He cannot do away with the direct result and consequences of our sin.

Another reason why some find the confessing of their sins to be a difficult matter is because when we stand before God and confess our transgressions, we must confess them in their entirety. We must tell the truth, the whole truth, and nothing but the truth. We cannot romanticize the transgression, and we cannot lessen our responsibility in the matter. We must be wholly honest and forthright with God, because He already knows the truth of it all.

We may be able to hide sin from men, but never from God. Even those who successfully hide their sins from others for a season are eventually found out, and this has happened on more than one occasion even within the church. David did not attempt to hide his sin from the Lord, or justify his sin before the Lord. He confessed, repented, and God honored his repentance.

Hebrews 4:13, "And there is no creature hidden from His sight, but all things are naked and open to the eyes of Him to whom we must give account."

If everyone who calls themselves a son or daughter of God would quote this verse upon waking, and upon going to sleep each night, there would be allot less sin within the house of God then there is presently.

The facts are grim. Seemingly, we are competing with the world in divorce rates, out of wedlock births, adultery, fornication, and every other thing God calls sin. It is because the truth of the aforementioned passage has not taken root in our hearts, and we view it only as theoretical rather than the absolute truth it is.

'All things are naked and open to the eyes of Him to who we must give account.'

Not only does God see all we do, we must give account for all we do. God is not playing games, even though we've been told He is. God does not make concessions nor does He negate His own justice. This is why Jesus had to die. This is why the Son of God had to hang on a cross, and expire before the mocking eyes of those of His time, because God cannot negate his own justice. We were all guilty, fated to be eternally separated from God, until Jesus came and bought us. He redeemed us and reconciled us unto the Father, not so we might continue in sin, but that we might be born again to eternal life in Him.

> *Luke 12:2-3, "For there is nothing covered that will not be revealed, nor hidden that will not be known. Therefore whatever you have spoken in the dark will be heard in the light, and what you have spoken in the ear in inner rooms will be proclaimed on the housetops."*

These were not the words of any ordinary man, but the words of Christ Jesus. No matter how well men might attempt to cover something, there is nothing covered that will not be revealed. No matter how well men might attempt to hide something, there is nothing hidden that will not be known.

Rather than waste our time and energy attempting to cover up and hide sin, it is far better to confess and repent that we may be forgiven. The Word of God tells us time and again that hiding or covering one's sin is impossible. Either we believe the Word and stop attempting what it clearly tells us we can never accomplish, or by our very actions imply our doubt of God's sovereign Scripture.

The Word of God remains ever true. Though men might like to change its meaning, render it irrelevant, deny the veracity of what it says, or do away with it altogether, the Word persists and subsists. Even when men somehow talk themselves into believing they've successfully circumvented the Word of God and justified their absence of repentance, there will come a day when everything will be laid bare, and He who knows all, sees all, and hears all, will judge righteously and justly.

David knew the God he served enough to humble himself and repent. He recognized the authority of God, the power of God, and the justice of God, knowing that in His righteousness God did not judge preferentially. Sin is ever lurking in the shadows. It is ever present throughout the lives of both wise men and fools, men of means and those of meager possessions, because sin does not care about the position or possessions of its prey as long as it is able to fell it.

Does the enemy take greater pleasure in bringing down one who is esteemed by his contemporaries as having been a man of principled righteousness? Perhaps, but sin itself has no such preferences. Although the enemy might revel at bringing down an officer in God's army, sin itself is content with whatever prey gets caught up in its web, whether they are a general, an officer, or a foot soldier.

Because we know sin is an equal opportunity destroyer, and because we know the enemy focuses his attacks upon those he perceives as a greater threat, our duty is to be ever watchful, ever vigilant, and ever aware of the enemy's ruthless and cunning tactics. When it comes to sin in the lives of believers, there is a misconception I want to dispel because I have run across it on occasion, and each time it is bothersome to me.

When an individual is in continual, habitual, and unrepentant sin, and they are exposed for what they had done, it is not the devil attacking them as they would like their followers to believe, it is God exposing them, so they either repent or walk away from the office which they held.

I've been in meetings where sincere individuals would stand and ask for prayer for a certain televangelist or preacher caught in adultery or worse, and they would always send their plea for prayer with, 'the devil's really attacking our brother, we must pray for him.' Sorry, no dice. Not going to happen. It's not the devil attacking him, it is God exposing him, because men's sins find them out and there is always an appointed time when God exposes them.

Psalm 90:8, "You have set our iniquities before You, our secret sins in the light of Your countenance."

Those things men hide in their hearts, thinking no one knows about, are set before God in the light of His countenance. He knows, and David knew this truth better than most preachers, pastors, deacons and elders do today. Men reach a certain position, they attain a certain office or title, then begin to think themselves beyond the reach of sin, beyond the tentacles of pride, of lust, of greed, and many other things which come peeking over the fence of our hearts to see if we are keeping watch. The enemy revels in the notion of a believer who having succumbed to sin refuses to confess and repent of the sin. Perhaps it's due to fear of what others might think of them if their sin is discovered, or the thought that they can get away with it this one time, but whatever the reason behind our absence of confession, as long as we are unrepentant, as long as we do not confess, the stain of sin will be evident.

1 John 1:9, "If we confess our sins, He is faithful and just to forgive us our sins and to cleanse us from all unrighteousness."

The forgiveness of our sin, and the cleansing from all unrighteousness, is contingent on whether or not we confess. God is faithful; of this there is no doubt. Faithful as He is, God is also constrained by His righteousness, and His righteousness dictates that in order for an individual to be forgiven and cleansed from unrighteousness, they must first confess their sin. David confessed his sin, and God forgave him. David poured out his heart to God, holding nothing back, and God extended grace to him.

Psalm 32:5, "I acknowledged my sin to You, and my iniquity I have not hidden. I said, 'I will confess my transgressions to the Lord.' And you forgave the iniquity of my sin. Selah."

Because he found forgiveness in the sight of God, David now had peace. The hand of the Lord was no longer heavy upon him, nor was his vitality turned to the drought of summer any longer. David confessed, and the burden was lifted. David confessed, and the weight was gone from upon his heart, and where once there was desperation and hopelessness, there was now peace and joy. David acknowledged his transgression. He confessed his sin, and did not attempt to hide his iniquity. He confessed his transgression to the Lord, and the Lord forgave the iniquity of his sin.

If someone followed a predetermined path and reached a predetermined destination, it is only logical to assume that if we follow the same path, we will likewise reach the same destination. David confessed and was forgiven. May we learn from the life of David, and if there is anything pressing down upon us, sapping us of our peace and joy, may we confess it and receive forgiveness.

There are many prayers David prayed within the pages of the Bible which are worthy of introspection and discussion, so it has proven quite difficult isolating two or three prayers to delve into. Since David was a man of prayer and a man dependent upon God, it is a worthwhile pursuit to understand what prayer meant to him. Yes, David prayed many prayers, but in the prayers we've discussed thus far, and the prayer we will discuss shortly, we come to understand what the act of prayer meant to David, and the value he placed upon it.

You can tell a lot about a man's relationship with God by how he values prayer. You can tell how strong or how weak one's intimacy with the Father is, by how often they bend the knee, and come before God in fellowship. No man ever stumbled because he prayed too much or too often or too long. No man ever stumbled because he spent too much time in fellowship with God or in God's presence. Men have stumbled, and continue to do so to this day because they neglect prayer, fellowship and intimacy with God, thereby allowing the enemy to worm his way into their hearts.

Thus far we have discussed David's prayer of thanks to God for having blessed him, David's prayer of repentance when he strayed, and now we will begin discussing David's prayers of recognition regarding God's sovereignty, as well as David's prayers of petition toward God.

Psalm 27:1, "The Lord is my light and my salvation; whom shall I fear? The Lord is the strength of my life; of whom shall I be afraid?"

When an individual comes to acknowledge that 'the Lord is,' their entire prayer life is transformed, as is the way in which they approach God. Three simple words: 'The Lord is' yet the declaration these three words make are forceful and all encompassing.

What have I to fear if the Lord is? What have I to be concerned with if the Lord is?

What is the Lord to you? To David, the Lord was his light, his salvation, and the strength of his life. David knew in whom he trusted, and why he trusted in Him. When David declares that 'the Lord is,' he isn't merely acknowledging the existence of God. David's declaration goes beyond mere knowledge of God's existence, to the realm of intimate knowledge of His attributes, and those things for which He was directly responsible in David's life.

David did not mistake what God had done for him with his own doings, or the doings of another. He did not take the credit for his strength or the light he possessed because he knew from whence they came. Beholding the tenderness, love, and heartfelt emotion with which David prayed, we come to realize the deep knowledge he possessed of God and the ways of God.

Psalm 27:10, "When my father and my mother forsake me, then the Lord will take care of me."

David recognized the perpetual faithfulness of God. He knew God would not abandon him in difficult times, when his enemies surrounded him, when his friends abandoned him, or when his own parents forsook him. Barring the requisite exceptions we can all agree that one's mother and father are likely the last individuals to abandon you. Though friends, brothers, acquaintances and spouses might forsake you, your mother and father will stick it out. David rests fully in the faithfulness of God, and the words of his prayer testify his absolute certainty that God will never abandon him.

Do we possess the same certainty as David did? Do we know to the depth of our heart that though our father and mother might forsake us the Lord will take care of us no matter what? As children of God this must be an unshakeable reality in our hearts. It matters not what we are going through, how many enemies we might have, how many legions of the enemy's minions stand against us, the Lord will take care of us.

The knowledge that God is ever present, ready to step in and take care of me makes my journey light and carefree even during the most treacherous moments. I know He is there, I know He will take care, what more can I desire?

David honors God from the depth of his heart, and acknowledges his dependence upon him. Oh, that we would learn to pray as David prayed, with sincerity and forthrightness giving glory to Him who is worthy of glory.

> *Psalm 18:1-3, "I will love You, O Lord, my strength. The Lord is my rock and my fortress and my deliverer; my God my strength, in whom I will trust. My shield and the horn of my salvation, my stronghold. I will call upon the Lord, who is worthy to be praised; so shall I be saved from my enemies."*

If we take the time to diligently study the book of Psalms, we come to realize David has prayers of praise, prayers of worship, prayers of thanks, prayers of confession, prayers of repentance, and even prayers of petition. With all the knowledge David possessed concerning God, we today ought to possess a greater knowledge of Him still, for He was revealed to us in greater measure and far more vividly through the Son Jesus Christ.

There is no excuse or justification for why the prayer lives of most professing Christians today are largely nonexistent. There is no excuse or justification for why so many professing Christians have a superficial knowledge at best. We can try to justify it to ourselves, and might even do a good enough job of appeasing and pacifying our conscience, but before God our excuses will not stand.

It's not that God will not open; it's that we never knocked. It's not that God cannot be found; it's that we never sought Him.

As flawed a figure as David is, it is undeniable he is also a highly relatable figure. Because there is so much of David within the pages of Scripture, it is nigh impossible not to find an aspect of David's life with which we can relate.

David was not a man who was embarrassed to ask for God's forgiveness when he stumbled. He was not one to attempt to blame it on someone else as Adam was wont to do, nor was he a man that skirted responsibility for his actions.

As such, one of David's most often prayed prayers of petition was petitioning God for forgiveness.

> Psalm 25:11, *"For Your name's sake, O Lord, pardon my iniquity, for it is great."*

> Psalm 25:18, *"Look on my affliction, and my pain, and forgive all my sins."*

Whenever David asked God for forgiveness, he admitted his guilt before God. One does not ask to be forgiven if they haven't done anything to be forgiven of. David knew of his own iniquity, he knew of his own sins, and when he prayed to God he did not attempt to minimize these things, or present himself before God as someone different than who he was.

When we petition God for forgiveness, what we are doing is asking God to be spared punishment. Being aware of our own guilt, we must likewise be aware of the punishment we are deserving of, and in our petitions for forgiveness we are asking God to pardon, and not punish us as we would rightly deserve. We serve a good God, a God who forgives when we ask for forgiveness, a God who pardons when we petition Him for a pardon. It is His good pleasure to forgive us, but we must repent and ask for forgiveness.

> Isaiah 43:25-26, *"I, even I, am He who blots out your transgressions for My own sake; and I will not remember your sins. Put Me in remembrance; Let us contend together; State your case that you may be acquitted."*

> Isaiah 44:22, *"I have blotted out, like a thick cloud, your transgressions, and like a cloud, your sins. Return to Me, for I have redeemed you."*

This is God speaking to His own people. He is not speaking to the godless, to the heathen, to those who never knew Him, but to those who know Him and have transgressed, and sinned. It is to His own that God makes the generous offer of blotting out their transgressions and their sins, if they put Him in remembrance, and state their case before Him.

Isaiah 55:7, "Let the wicked forsake his way, and the un-righteous man his thoughts; let him return to the Lord, and He will have mercy on him; and to our God, for He will abundantly pardon."

David knew of God's requirements when he came before Him asking for forgiveness. David knew that true repentance required the forsaking of one's way, and a return to the Lord, who would then have mercy. Just saying we're sorry or asking for forgiveness in our prayers is not sufficient in and of itself. What God requires of us, is a turning, a forsaking of our wicked ways, and an embracing of righteousness and sanctification. God does not forgive just so we return to the mire from which He plucked us. He does not cleanse us, and give us white garments just so we get them muddy again, returning to our former thoughts, desires and lusts. Not only does David pray that his iniquities and sins be forgiven him, he also prays to be forgiven of his secret faults and presumptuous sins.

Psalm 19:12-13, "Who can understand his errors? Cleanse me from secret faults. Keep back Your servant also from presumptuous sins; Let them not have dominion over me. Then I shall be blameless, and I shall be innocent of great transgression."

There are intentional, willful sins, transgressions men commit knowing full well exactly what they are doing, then there are unintentional sins, or sins committed through error. David repents and asks forgiveness for his intentional sins, but also for his unintentional sins. Yes, the notion of unintentional sin is a Biblical one, and we find it within the pages of Scripture.

Leviticus 4:1-2, "Now the Lord spoke to Moses, saying, 'speak to the children of Israel, saying: 'If a person sins unintentionally against any of the commandments of the Lord in anything which out not to be done, and does any of them, if the anointed priest sins, bringing guilt on the people, then let him offer to the Lord for his sin which he has sinned a young bull without blemish as a sin offering."

The notion of unintentional sin is mentioned no less than six times within this chapter alone, and God was aware of this facet of human existence, and he included it in His Word. There are many today within the household of faith who practice unintentional sin, because they are unaware of the fact that God considers what they are doing sinful. Ignorance of God's Word begets unintentional sin, and I've heard people saying 'I didn't know that was a sin,' far too often within many a congregation.

The consequence of not defining what God considers sin, the consequence of not preaching against sin, is myriads of men and women who are sinning unintentionally because no one ever told them their practice was sinful. When we clearly define what is acceptable and what is not acceptable, what is sin and what isn't sin, then at least we know we've done our part, and those who have heard our words have no excuse for not adhering to the Word of the living God.

It is neither loving nor tolerant to see someone calling themselves a believer, practicing what the Bible clearly defines as sinful, and not pointing it out to them. One of the most loving things God can do for us as His children, is convict us of our unintentional sins, because with each thing God convicts us of, we are that much closer to becoming that which God had intended us to be.

Within the pages of Scripture, God has been compared to a potter who molds the clay in the shape He desires, but who also places the molded clay into the furnace to make it strong and cause it to retain its shape. Every time God convicts us of something, He is placing us into the furnace, not only forming us into the image He desires us to be, but making us stronger by removing impurities and uncleanness.

As with many a biblical precept and principle, we've twisted the notion of chastening within the modern day church, to the point that it is now an unwelcome and undesired event rather than the good and positive thing the Bible tells us it is. It is for our own good that God convicts us. It is for our own good that God chastens us, and we must respond to His chastening and conviction with all requisite haste.

Acts 17:30-31, "Truly, these times of ignorance God overlooked, but now commands all men everywhere to repent, because

He has appointed a day on which He will judge the world in righteousness by the Man whom He has ordained. He has given assurance of this to all by raising Him from the dead."

Although God overlooks our times of ignorance, when an unintentional sin is revealed to us, when God makes it known whether through His Word or through His servants, it is incumbent upon us to repent of it. We come before God with our prayers of repentance as David did, asking God to forgive all that would stand as a stumbling block between ourselves and His glory. We ask God for forgiveness, knowing He is faithful to forgive, knowing He is just to render to each according to His righteousness, and to mend the broken and contrite heart when it cries out to Him.

Another of David's prayers which has been close to my heart since first reading the passage in the book of Psalms many years ago—and a prayer I often repeat myself during my time with the Lord—is for a closer and more profound spiritual walk with God.

David was wise enough to know that absent a clean heart and a steadfast spirit, one cannot have a true, lasting, vibrant and profound spiritual walk with God. As such, David's prayer was not for the thing itself, but for the virtues which would facilitate the thing in his life. David did not pray for a closer spiritual walk, he prayed for the steadfastness and clean heart which he knew would inevitably bring him closer to the Lord.

Psalm 51:10, "Create in me a clean heart, O God, and renew a steadfast spirit within me."

Seeing as having a clean heart is of great import, what does having a clean heart entail?

Personally I believe a clean heart is a heart made clean by the blood of Christ, but also a heart which is sincere in all its doings, wherein what is in our heart and what is on our lips are one and the same thing. If there is conflict between what is in our hearts and what is on our lips, if we think one thing and speak another, then our hearts are not clean.

A clean heart begins from within. It is something which cannot be taught, it is something for which no manual exists. It is a work between us and God, facilitated by our willingness to forego our own will and be wholly submitted to His authority.

Psalm 24:3-4, "Who may ascend into the hill of the Lord? Or who may stand in His holy place? He who has clean hands and a pure heart, who has not lifted up his soul to an idol, nor sworn deceitfully."

Who can stand in God's holy place? The Word of God is very specific as to the group of individuals who will ascend into the hill of the Lord and stand in His holy place. By what David tells us via the inspiration of the Holy Spirit, we realize that it has nothing to do with one's denomination, age, gender, or nationality, but with whether or not they have clean hands, a pure heart, have not lifted their soul to an idol, or sworn deceitfully.

Through Christ and His shed blood we are transformed into such individuals, we are renewed, born again, having pure hearts where once our hearts were evil, having clean hands where once our hands were stained.

As we follow this train of thought to its rightful conclusion, we also come to understand that though some might call themselves brothers or sisters, though some might call themselves believers, they are believers in name only because their hands have not been made clean, nor have their hearts been purified. Countless souls today actively practice idolatry and lift up their souls to idols, all the while claiming to be faithful followers of Christ.

More could be said, but I will refrain, because we are studying the prayer life of David, and not all the idols idolatrous idolaters worship in our day and age.

The other thing David prayed for was a steadfast spirit.

In order to be steadfast, one needs some sort of trouble or difficulty, because the definition of steadfastness is loyalty in the face of said trouble or difficulty. Men can claim to be steadfast, but until their season of trouble comes they are but mere blustering braggarts, going about inflating their own egos. When we pray for a steadfast spirit, we are praying for God to give us the boldness, the courage, the forthrightness, and loyalty to withstand the attacks of the enemy, to hold our position and to stand our ground.

Pray for a steadfast spirit only once you've understood what it all entails, and are prepared to be on the frontline of the battle. A steadfast spirit implies that you will meet the enemy head on when others are fleeing, that you will stand your ground when others are retreating, and that you will advance the cause of the kingdom of God when others are about their own business.

Possessing a steadfast spirit goes beyond having the boldness to stand one's ground against the enemy. When we possess a steadfast spirit, we are not swayed by new winds of doctrine and teaching as so many seem to be, but rather, we stand on the rock that is Christ, unmoved, unshaken, unperturbed and undistracted by the countless voices attempting to lead us astray. It is because so few possess steadfastness that so many go from one doctrine to another, ever searching but never finding what they are searching for.

We have the Word of God as the final authority in matters concerning the spiritual, and when we are steadfast we defer to the Bible rather than to our denominations, and remain on the narrow path of faith regardless of how many voices would attempt to beguile us to the contrary. Rather than learn to be dependent upon the guidance, inspiration and urging of the Holy Spirit as David had, we are taught by men who ought to know better that our opinions, feelings and preferences supersede the Holy Spirit's leadings, and as such He can readily be ignored and marginalized.

David understood the importance of having the Spirit of God ever present in his life. He understood the importance of walking led by the Spirit and prayed in earnest that God would not remove His Spirit from him.

Psalm 51:11-13, "Do not cast me away from Your presence, and do not take Your Holy Spirit from me. Restore to me the joy of Your salvation, and uphold me with Your generous Spirit. Then I will teach transgressors Your ways, and sinners shall be converted to You."

The presence of the Holy Spirit in his life was foremost on David's mind and heart. He realized the one thing he could not live without, and so prayed that God would not take it from him. David knew he could live without his crown, his kingdom, his wealth, his accolades, his army and his reputation, but he could not live without the Holy Spirit, and so prayed this sobering prayer.

David also realizes what God desires of those who call themselves His children is not simply sacrifice, although bringing a sacrifice would be a far easier task than walking in the will of God as He commands us to do. We can offer up tokens, we can offer up trinkets, we can offer up things men would prize and see as valuable, but as long as we do not offer up our hearts, as long as we do not offer up ourselves in our entirety, we fall short of doing what is pleasing in the sight of God.

I realize full well that those who would have your coin and your possessions far outnumber those who would have you surrender your heart to God, but the truth doesn't always lie with the majority, nor does righteousness or wisdom for that matter.

Psalm 51:16-17, "For You do not desire sacrifice, or else I would give it; You do not delight in burnt offering. The sacrifices of God are a broken spirit, a broken and contrite heart – these, O God, You will not despise."

David had realized the futility of half measures when it came to the things of God. He realized that men of unclean hands bringing sacrifice before God was something He despised, but also that God would honor a broken spirit and a broken and contrite heart. Imperfect as David might have been, he loved the Lord, he loved the house of the Lord, and he loved the way of the Lord. It is this burning love for God that must motivate us, drive us, and compel us to seek His will in all we do.

David set out two possible paths his son Solomon could have taken, and encouraged him to choose the right path. If Solomon sought God, David confirmed the truth that Solomon would indeed find Him. If however he chose to forsake God, then God would cast him off forever. Although he had reached the heights of power, although there was not a man with more authority than him in the entire kingdom, David still humbled himself and acknowledged his need for God, His Holy Spirit, and his continued guidance.

Psalm 25:4-5, "Show me Your ways, O Lord; teach me Your paths. Lead me in Your truth and teach me, for You are the God of my salvation on You I wait all day."

Pray for God's revelation and you shall have it. Pray that He show you His ways, and He will. Pray that He teaches you His paths, and you will see Him illuminate the way, for He is a good and loving

God whose desire is always a more sanctified you. God's promises remain ever true, and He promised that if we asked to be led in His truth and taught by Him, He would teach us and lead us.

Isaiah 30:21, "Your ears shall hear a word behind you, saying, 'This is the way, walk in it.' Whenever you turn to the right hand or whenever you turn to the left."

As David's knowledge of God grew his trust and dependence upon God grew in equal proportion. The more of God we come to know, the more we come to realize just how fragile, powerless and small we really are, and how great, omnipotent and all-encompassing our God is. When we come to know God, we do not spend less time in His presence but more, we do not desire less of Him, but more. Knowledge of God only fuels a desire for more of Him in our lives, and eventually we come to that place as David did so long ago, where we realize, absent His presence in our lives and hearts, it will be impossible for us to breathe one more breath.

David was at the end of his journey here on earth. In a short while he would return to the earth from whence he came, and he begins leaving charges to Israel, as well as to his son Solomon. As his parting words to his son Solomon, David encourages him not to seek fame, not to seek fortune, not to seek power, but to seek to know the God of his father. Everything else in this world pales in comparison to man's need to know God personally.

1 Chronicles 28:9, "As for you, my son Solomon, know the God of your father, and serve Him with a loyal heart and with a willing mind; for the Lord searches all hearts and understands all the intent of the thoughts. If you seek Him, He will be found by you; but if you forsake Him, He will cast you off forever."

We have learned much from the prayer of David, and my hope is that we apply what we have learned to our daily time of devotion and fellowship in the presence of God.

OTHER BOOKS BY MICHAEL BOLDEA, JR.

The Holy Spirit: Power, Presence, and Purpose
Fundamental Doctrines: Understanding the Elementary Principles of Christ
When Ye Pray: The Anatomy of Prayer – Book One
365 Thoughts Meditations & Words of Wisdom

Made in the USA
Middletown, DE
28 January 2017